ASYMMETRIC ADVANTAGE

ASYMMETRIC ADVANTAGE

HOW STARTUP LEADERS
CAN GET COMFORTABLE
BEING UNCOMFORTABLE

JASON VAN DER SCHYFF

LIONCREST
PUBLISHING

Copyright © 2021 Jason Van der Schyff

All right reserved.

Asymmetric Advantage:
How Startup Leaders Can Get Comfortable Being Uncomfortable

Hardcover ISBN: 978-1-5445-2351-4
Paperback ISBN: 978-1-5445-2352-1
eBook ISBN: 978-1-5445-2353-8

CONTENTS

Author's Note
vii

Introduction
ix

Chapter 1
Asymmetric Advantage
1

Chapter 2
Get Shit Done
15

Chapter 3
Balance and Pressure
29

Chapter 4
Culture
41

Chapter 5
Scaling
59

Chapter 6
Leadership
75

Chapter 7
Find Your Replacement
95

Chapter 8
Step Up
109

Conclusion
119

Acknowledgments
129

AUTHOR'S NOTE

Some of the company and individual names have been changed to protect the innocent—or the guilty.

INTRODUCTION

QUIBI WAS A STREAMING SERVICE CREATED WITH MOBILE DEVICES IN MIND, and there is really no reason it should have failed. It launched when we were all trapped at home at the height of quarantine; we even ran out of stuff to watch. But the creators of Quibi had too much cash, too much power at the start. Imagine a newborn baby with arms like Dwayne "The Rock" Johnson. It's not going to know what to do with them, and someone's bound to get hurt.

The creators didn't grow the platform organically; they basically tried to buy growth. They spent a billion dollars commissioning content: 170–180 shows and 8,000 episodes, which is excessive, even by Netflix's standards. Their aim was shorter content designed for shorter attention spans (and wrist stamina). But there was just no way people could get through all the content. They should have created less content with much better quality. If they had done this, they would have at least made it through the first year.[1]

Quibi tried to be the new Netflix right off the bat but found it was out of its depth. I've found that's a common issue with tech-related startups: they try to operate like a large company,

---

[1] Where does exclusive content go when it dies? Cloud Nine?

like they're already a big shot, but then they flop anyway. But business leaders want to read books about how to be the next Google or Facebook; they want to know how to copy someone else's success. Just to make a point, here are some rapid-fire lessons from Google, Facebook, Netflix, and more that people try (and fail) to implement in their own businesses.

The Big-Tech Lessons

Leaders believe *if a process works in one successful business, why wouldn't it work in ours?* They try to replicate a handful of well-known big-tech processes and procedures and are puzzled when they don't become the next Google. The problem lies in not understanding why something is being done. Without knowing the full reasoning behind a process—and knowing how it applies to *your* business—implementation fails. Most leaders, perhaps even you, have attempted to copy one or more of the following processes, with less than stellar results.

Make Meetings More Productive: Google meetings start on time, and their cue to finish is people knocking on the door at the top of the hour. Meetings do not go over the allotted time at Google. Similarly, Amazon says, "If you don't have an agenda, then you don't have a meeting." Using these principles, both companies keep their meetings productive. In smaller companies, however, a meeting may need to be longer. It may need to go as long as it takes. In the beginning, you're brainstorming, thinking big picture, instead of checking boxes. Rushing meetings at the start could stifle your creativity.

Build a Brand That Makes You Stand Out: Yahoo! and Ask Jeeves were relatively successful before Google made a comprehensive brand name for itself. With Google Suites came the perpetuated notion that Google was a household name, one people could trust for the answers. If newer companies are too focused on brand, however, they could forget to create a worthwhile product. (That sounds stupid, but I've seen it happen, firsthand.)

Startups Can Be Brave: "Move fast and break things" is a common motto for startup tech agencies, and Facebook has adapted it so well that it includes "move fast" as one of its core cultural values on its website. They broke into the social media game, knocked MySpace right out of orbit, and became the most used platform. The current model is unrecognizable from "The Facebook," yet the product leaves its customers feeling more satisfied than not. But as a new company, your intention matters. If you're trying to black out the competition before you even have a platform to compete with, you're going to lose.

Keep People on Your Platform: Netflix enabled people to binge-watch their favorite shows, and people were already grateful for that. (Well, not Blockbuster or Redbox, but everyone else.) By creating new, exclusive content, they created lifetime loyalists. They kept customers streaming and satisfied. Likewise, Amazon expanded from an online bookstore to a company that could give its customers everything from A to Z (in two days or less). They even came up with their own streaming service, one that customers could only access from the same site they used to buy toilet paper in bulk. I've already wagged my finger at companies who try to get ahead of their skis on this.

Have a Culture Fit for Creatives: Netflix's culture is a factory for creativity: employees are encouraged to share their ideas "openly, broadly, and deliberately" as well as "avoid rules," according to the Culture page on their website. Netflix recognizes that the magic happens when the people on the ground are free to do as they please. This public view works great for Netflix, but the boundaries aren't available for public access.

These Lessons Aren't for You

Those big-tech lessons? They're not what this book is about.

You may look up to the Big Four, also known as Tech Giants or Four Horsemen, and it's tempting to try to emulate their practices, believing you'll find the same success by doing so. Let me tell you the truth: you don't have to be like Google, Facebook, Amazon, Apple, or any other promising tech company.

As a business leader, you want to hurry up and solve your problems, so you likely look to other companies' solutions. You ask, *What is Google doing? How does Netflix conduct their culture? How did Facebook get so big?* But their solutions are for someone else's problems, not yours. If you're just a parrot, echoing other people's solutions, you won't develop the skill to solve problems for yourself. You need to sit with your own business's issues to discover your own solutions. *You have to get comfortable being uncomfortable.* When you're able to do this, you may find that some of your "problems" actually present a unique advantage.

I can't tell you how to solve your problems, but I can point out the possible origin of these problems and alleviate the temptation to just do what the cool kids are doing. I can show you why their solutions paid off for their own unique problems, and how you can use this information to devise your own unique solutions—your own asymmetric advantage. You'll accomplish far more. When you follow your asymmetric advantage, you can create an ideal company culture, work and vacation like the rich (even if you're not), scale with intention, lead and create a new wave of leaders, and then go forth and *do the thing*.

My goal is that this will be the last book you read before starting your own tech-related startup or seizing the leadership role you've been given. After reading this book, you should have all the tools and confidence you need to get shit done and be the badass you've always dreamed of being.

I've Walked in Your Shoes

Why do you want to listen to some guy tell you not to do what successful companies are doing? What's the appeal there? Some sharks might adopt this facade, hoping you'll leave these free lessons of success on the table, specifically so you'll fail in business, which would effectively eliminate you as competition.

My goal here is to do the opposite: to keep you from getting wrapped up in other people's success stories. I've benefited from great mentors. Not everyone has access to those, but everyone can access a book. Let me be a mentor to you.

If you believe these lessons are a surefire way to become successful in your business, and then you fail anyway, you're going to have a much harder time getting back up. And it's the getting back up that's crucial for success.

I have twenty years of experience in the technology industry. I have gone from product manager to director of product marketing to VP of marketing and operations and beyond. I'm now the Chief Operations Officer of PiedPiper, which creates appliances that connect securely to private and public data centers.

Although I have been with PiedPiper since its conception, I worked my way up to COO, serving first as Director of Operations, then as VP of Operations. I have always had a company-first vision, and that focus has trickled down to garner my personal success.

I began building my asymmetric advantage long ago. I started out making websites for people in high school. Thanks to my parents, I had early access to the internet and was curious enough about it to learn HTML. I built the website for my school, which wasn't beautiful but was easy enough to navigate—and made five grand in the process. That's nothing to sneeze at for a teenager, and that financial success encouraged me to start my first company.

It may surprise you to learn that I never went to college. And by that, I do not mean that I got into Harvard and used my connections and prestige to quit before graduating and make a worldwide social media platform. I mean, I didn't attend college at all, let alone rub elbows with Ivy League-ers or go on to get an MBA like many of my competitors. By all accounts, I should be a big fat failure right now. But I'm not. And there's a reason for that.

Unburdened by traditional education, I never learned *what* to think. I didn't have any bad habits to unlearn. I broke a lot of programming, formatting, and design rules to explore my creativity freely. Despite many instances of failing (which you'll get some close-ups on during the course of this book, don't worry), my lack of education was not a disadvantage but was my asymmetric advantage, something that looked like a sign of my failure but ended up being a guiding light toward my success. Now, I want to help you create your own asymmetric advantage.

Stop Trying to Steal Success

Essentially, every business book ever written approaches success through one of two avenues:

1. A montage of company failures to illustrate success by spotlighting its absence (a "DON'T" list), or

2. A *Rocky*-style inspirational "You Can Do It Too!" string of business achievements.

There will be plenty of the former in this book—but not so you can step over these company corpses like debris on your own path to success. You have more in common with these companies than you realize. My job isn't to point out the failures of others so that you can avoid them. It's to show you what happens when people try to steal someone else's success. We'll be looking at companies that:

- Tried to implement too much consumer feedback into their product, making it a product for no one instead of a product for their intended audience (everyone)

- Blew through their budgets on the wrong things, trying to look like one of the Big Kids before they were tall enough to ride this ride

- Forced connection between team members through happy-hour/work-related meetings at times that were inconvenient for most of the people on the ground

- Catered to the pride of C-suite members instead of recognizing the bilateral nature of communication between leaders and team members

Some of these companies had a great idea but went bankrupt before getting to share it with the world. Others got off the ground with their products but failed at lightning speed because they were caught up in perfectionism.

Most of the issues with these companies boil down to one or more of three core problem areas:

- People

- Money

- Experience

And while these epic-fail montages, complete with sloppy YouTube transitions and tacky sound effects, are great for telling business leaders what not to do in business, they don't really help them understand what *to do* if they have already fallen prey to one of the above problems.

That's why many business leaders prefer the second avenue toward illustrating business success: the inspirational montage, the camera following a hugely successful tech bro up the stairs while he punches his invisible company problems out of his way on the path toward success.

Your origin story, however, doesn't need to match those high-profile execs'. You don't have to live in the Bay Area to be successful in tech. You can carve a path for yourself on your own grind. Let's begin to discover your asymmetric advantage.

CHAPTER 1

ASYMMETRIC ADVANTAGE

WHEN YOU READ THE NAME "SQUIDWORKS," DOES IT RING A BELL? Probably not. SquidWorks was a small tech company that built electronics and performed mechanical engineering and injection molding. They were a company made up of three guys who worked alone in a warehouse. But even though they were a much smaller company, they won a pretty big client over a big, scary defense contractor, one that was endorsed by a former shady vice president.

And we're not talking just any client here. We're talking about the US Air Force—specifically, the Space and Missile Defense Command, which is important to note because it sounds way cooler.

The Space Command needed a rock, or something that resembled a rock, to serve as a covert weather station. Sometimes they needed to send a small patrol of Army-Marine-SEALs to a site in Afghanistan, so they needed a device that could ensure they wouldn't accidentally fly a helicopter into the Taliban. Sending six or more special forces soldiers anywhere is a pretty expensive endeavor, not to mention dangerous. They needed something that could be installed (just once); wake up on demand or on a schedule; measure wind speed, wind direction, and the proximity of lightning; and send that information through a satellite network to the Department of Defense. And do all of that in a way that wouldn't attract the attention of the enemy.

Space Command went to one of the big companies—you know, the ones that make a killing off of war—and was like, "This is what we need. Make it happen." The WarMonger company ten-foured that information, but the product they designed was basically a weather *boulder* instead of a rock—it simply wasn't practical. The air force needed to be able to transport this weather station inconspicuously; they wanted something handheld. They lost multiple millions of dollars on that project.

Cue SquidWorks, who had some experience in space communication. Space Command presented them with WarMonger's failed project and said, "Can you fix this in three months?" The engineers at SquidWorks charged this gratuitously funded government program a mere $150,000 to do the whole project, and they thought that was pretty good because $150K split three ways is still a year's salary for some people.

After doing some investigating, SquidWorks was like, "Is a rock really the best thing? What if we made this into a camouflaged cylinder that goes on a tripod? You don't want to measure weather on the ground, anyway; you won't get an accurate reading on the wind." They connected with a company in Silicon Valley that had built the world's smallest lightning sensor. WarMonger tried to use a sensor to measure lightning to the nearest meter, but SquidWorks knew it didn't need to be that specific. The air force just didn't want to be *surprised* by lightning in a helicopter; they just needed to know, "Is there lightning *around*?"

Because they had money and a larger workforce, WarMonger divided the work and pieced everything together at the end, which is why they ended up with a boulder instead of spy hardware after nine months and millions of dollars spent. SquidWorks made a product that the client was, ultimately, all the more satisfied with—*because* they approached the problem precisely the opposite way.

Discover Your Asymmetric Advantage

WarMonger should have been the better candidate for the air force's project. They had more manpower, more clout, and more resources. You would think that all those great minds would have produced a satisfactory product. But it's exactly because they had such a big team that they missed the mark on the portable weather station. They broke the project up into smaller tasks and assigned those to specialists, who then did not communicate well enough with one another. SquidWorks, on the other hand, nurtured an intimate space conducive to sharing ideas and communicating the results of failed experiments.

To any onlookers, SquidWorks's team size would have been considered a disadvantage, especially when compared to WarMonger's resources. But this alleged weakness is exactly what enabled them to succeed. This is what I call an **asymmetric advantage**.

You can turn any disadvantage into an asymmetric advantage if you shift your mindset about it. Perception is powerful. You've probably heard the saying, "If you think you can't, then you can't," and that's cliché at this point, but clichés enter our vernacular for a reason: they're true.

WarMonger wasn't open to a different perspective. We're told what to do and how to do things a lot in our lives, and sometimes you have to break those assumptions to come up with something that actually does the job. That sometimes requires that horrible "think outside the box" advice that we've all heard before, but how do you make yourself think outside the box? To me, it requires tenacity. If you accept the status quo, that's fine, I guess, but you'll never see outside the box, let alone embody that mindset to make real, lasting change in your business. But if you reject the status quo and embrace tenacity, you can start doing more impressive things in your line of work.

You need to understand that you do not need to mirror the tactics of lizard people like Mark Zuckerberg or some other thirty-under-thirty member. Specifically, you should *not* do this. It will not work out for you—not because your team is too small or you don't have enough money or whatever, but because your business is not Facebook or Google. What works for Facebook and Google is all good and fine, but they had to discover what worked for them and what didn't, just like you're going to have to do for your own business.

To help you stop asking yourself, "WWSJD?" ("What Would Steve Jobs Do?") you have to discover your own asymmetric advantage.

Here's a list of all the things that could supposedly keep you from succeeding in your business:

- Your teeny team size
- Lack of formal education
- Inexperience
- Sporadic résumé
- Low (or nonexistent) funds
- Too many good ideas (and poor focus)

Ultimately, these things boil down to three categories: people, money, and experience. Your team is made up of people; the culture depends on people; your leadership lords over people. Experience can be understood in the traditional sense or come in the way of education. Money is a dark cloud over everything, waiting for you to do a rain dance. And, of course, some people have to dance harder than others.

Let's take a look.

PEOPLE

Marissa Mayer was a product manager at Google, got given a killer product, and just crushed it. Then, the next thing you know she's the CEO of Yahoo!. She skipped ten steps, and suddenly, she's the leader of an entire organization—of people, not a lifeless product. No one became a public company CEO as fast in history as she did. Marissa inherited this dumpster fire of a company and the immense pressure to somehow revive it, an impossible task for most people, let alone someone with no C-suite leadership experience.

Marissa Mayer had proven to be a talented executive at Google, and she (and the Yahoo! board) believed that she was ready to step up, but it was a disaster in the long term. If you want to jump ahead ten steps at once in your career, go for it, but you also need to know what you don't know. For example, you can be a bit of an ass when you're a project manager, but you kind of can't be when you're the CEO. Typically, when people get uncomfortable, we resort to behavior that we're used to, that we *are* comfortable with, but if we have to adapt to our *new* environment, what got us here won't get us there. I believe she should have come in asking questions, not making demands. She didn't establish trust with her team members, so no one bought into her vision for the company. It wasn't like Zuckerberg where it was his way or the highway, and he didn't really give a shit what anyone thought about his dictatorship—because, you know, *he invented the product*. She got a bit big for her boots, if you like. Without this collective consciousness working to solve the same problem in the same way, there was no way for her to win. She did an awesome job at Google but a terrible job at Yahoo!.

I'm not trying to kick her while she's down. My view has always been that what happened to her was massively unfair because the Yahoo! board should have known better. They should have recognized what type of leader they required in their hour of need, and they didn't and Mayer took the brunt of it. She was a brand-new leader, with her fresh faults on display for all to see. She went from *zero to hero* at Google to *zero to a hundred* at Yahoo!. All we need to do as leaders is go from zero to one. In a big company, it's common to not even make it to one.

I view myself very much at this point in my career as a zero-to-one guy. I'm the guy who works out how to do it. Even if I don't know anything about it, I just go and learn about it and then hopefully scale it to a size that's big enough for my needs. If there's something that needs to be done in a small company, it doesn't matter if it's your job or not, it just has to be done. There is no finance team when there's three of you, and someone has to do the tax return. You can't not do it. So, the pro of having a small team is that you need fewer people to buy into your vision, but you also need to be prepared to do more work because you don't have people to delegate to. But you have to remember that you can't just order people around as your team grows either.

I didn't gain my knowledge of team (and, therefore, people) management from big-tech companies. Those giants don't care about their team members (case in point, Yahoo!). You've heard about people who cry at their desks at Amazon? That's real. Learn your soft skills from your small team, which is an advantage, for your intents and purposes, not a disadvantage at all.

EXPERIENCE

We have to break the notion that the only place you get educated is at a school. Now, we don't want a bunch of doctors who learn by trial and error, so there are good bits of formal education. At the end of the day, the bulk of people do go to college, and the next wave of business leaders have generally gone to college.

I don't necessarily want to be the guy who says, "Don't go to college. It's a waste of time and money." I was lucky: I had one parent who went to college and one parent who didn't, and they both ended up being successful people, both CEOs in the not-for-profit sector. To me, it was clear that you didn't *have* to go to college to be successful, despite what many millennials were taught growing up. It wasn't a prerequisite, though I also knew one path is definitely easier than the other. I was biased to my stepdad's approach on life (no college), but my father had an MBA, so it wasn't like I came from a family where college wasn't valued. I just essentially made the decision that even though I was accepted into college, I wouldn't go. I would go off and work instead.

You don't have to go on to get a higher education to be the best startup leader you can be—and, despite the popular belief of the past decade, Zuckerberg's success, despite not graduating from Harvard, *is not* an example of this truth. It doesn't matter that Zuckerberg didn't graduate from Harvard. The point is that he was accepted into and went to Harvard. Before that, he attended elitist schools that led to Harvard, and his family were wealthy. He didn't exactly grow up roughin' it. He's not Jenny from the Block: he never "had a little." What I mean is, Zuckerberg's "education" was his connections, and because he came from money and prestige from the start, he had easier access to those resources. We shouldn't compare ourselves to that sweaty, pale-faced, dead-eyed billionaire because we have souls. Just kidding—we shouldn't compare ourselves because our backgrounds are different from his, and that's okay.

I like to tell people I got my "grad school diploma" when I successfully navigated a lawsuit at a company I worked at prior to PiedPiper—except in a way, it was better than an MBA education because they don't teach you about lawsuits in business school. I've read most of the business school books because I figured that was cheaper than going to business school. They tell you the principles, but you don't know anything until you do it. In that process, I learned way more than I would ever have imagined around mitigation motion law.

My team and I had spun up a little brand, and we ended up, after two years, getting a cease-and-desist letter (from a 900-pound gorilla with a history of predatory lawsuits) against infringement of one of their trademarks. So, we lawyered it up, and we countersued them, antitrust. In a way, they never formally sued us because they just followed the cease and desist. We actually sued *them*.

I suddenly had to learn a massive amount of investment law and HR law and dust off my corporate finance books. Now, I was the guy who was approving the finances every month to the company, and I went from being a contributor to holding up the fall.

So, don't worry if you do or don't have formal education. Just be open and always learning. If you stop pushing yourself to learn, then you can't expect great or amazing things to happen. Knowledge isn't going to just pop into you. People get lucky for sure, but most people have to work really, really hard to get the things that they have or be in the position that they're in. It's less about getting a formal education and more about being open to being educated in the real world.

MONEY

More money definitely makes life easier, but capital can also kill. People generally get pretty sloppy with money, especially when it's not their money. In a lot of instances, investors really like it when they see people bootstrap their initial efforts. "Wow, you did this all by yourself?" they imply. "You got all the way here, and now, I'm going to give you money like the Rockettes."

All of the companies that raise a bunch of money—the first thing they go and do is buy a whole bunch of stupid shit like those chairs by Herman Miller. They're a thousand bucks a pop or something, which is surprisingly midrange for an office chair. When startups get funding, they manage to convince themselves that thousand-dollar chairs are necessary. Part of the brand.

"Oh, we've got fifty people? Let's go and buy fifty of these chairs because we've got $50,000 to blow, so why not? Let's get fancy."

There's a joke in the Bay Area: if you buy those chairs new, it's like a kiss of death. You might as well start digging a hole in the ground, so your company has a place to rest when it goes under.

I'll be real with you and say we have those chairs at PiedPiper, but I buy them used at $450 each—from all of the startups that bought them new and then promptly went bust. We get the same result. It's the same chair. It's still made in the same factory in Illinois, nothing different about it whatsoever. The point is, you don't have to go and do the stupid thing when you get money.

About five years ago, a software code repository company got bought by Microsoft for some obscene amount of money, but before that, they got a bunch of press coverage because they built a replica of the oval office in their office building. They just replaced the US seal with their own logo, but other than that, it was a pretty impressive model of the real thing. It cost them stupid money, and for what? Spending that money ultimately meant that their business didn't succeed. Was it worth it? Of course not.

Money in the form of oval offices and thousand-dollar chairs doesn't lead you to success. Full stop. They don't lead to the culture that you're trying to foster by being one of the big guys. If you're smart, that will come in time. You can get big, and you can do all of that stupid stuff, but it just doesn't make a difference in the early stages of the company. At least, not in the way you want it to.

Having money isn't enough; it's about where we spend the money and what we spend it on. People are the most important part of setting up a company and scaling it. Great ideas don't come out of money. They come out of people, so spend money on people, not things.

When I was working at a smaller company, we had enough money for the three of us to fly from San Francisco to Vegas to attend this conference for Diving Equipment and Association (DEMA), which is the diving equipment manufacturers association. At this stage, let's just say the bank accounts collectively were not particularly healthy. We had $500 between us, and we spent the money on nineteen-dollar-a-night hotel rooms (you can imagine the quality) and the bill to take a big prospective client out for dinner. We literally had nothing else; if we didn't land this client, we were done. The only way we were possibly going to get any business in the short term was to convince this guy to buy the product that we prototyped. It really was an all-in move. If it hadn't worked, we'd have been flying back to San Francisco looking for jobs on the plane. But because we were willing to take a chance with the very small amount of money we had, we landed the client and put in the full work on the in-flight WiFi.

Having a lot of money or a little shouldn't impact your business decisions. If you have something special and you believe in your company, there's a good chance you'll make it; if you stay in the mindset that your finances mean you're a failure from the start, then you'll never succeed.

What Happened to SquidWorks?

SquidWorks started out making crazy, ridiculous date scuba diving equipment, because there's nothing like breathing all these exotic gases to get your heart rate pounding out of both fear and attraction to your lover. No one in the industry was building the products that SquidWorks thought should be built, and the most dangerous thing in the world is three engineers with a lot of time on their hands.

They traveled a lot, and they didn't exactly have the money for it. They had $500 in a bank account at one point and spent $495 to get to a trade show and take a customer out for dinner in the hopes of landing a new client that would breathe life into their scuba tanks.

The three guys were scuba divers themselves and had a mutual friend from diving, who had a brother-in-law at the Future Soldier Program at the US Army—yeah, even small businesses thrive on who they know. "The next time he's in town," he said, "we should all go out to lunch." They made plans; the day came; they met the guy. The army guy says, "Could you guys do some specialized stuff for us?"

Then that connection led to another and boom: weather rock. Space station. Client landed and money earned.

Some other things that happened inside SquidWorks meant that they got the opportunity to land a couple hundred thousand dollars from a different client. It would involve a sister company of theirs, and some of the guys there came to them and said, "You came up with this rock-star idea in the first place. You were already shareholders in the company. Could we do some merger, where everything is the same, but we're being run out of the SquidWorks office too?" Why not? It was just these three engineers, so one said to the others, "Hey, can you guys, starting January one, basically put on a different T-shirt and start winding SquidWorks down? Let's make PiedPiper worth our while, so we don't need to keep chasing quarter-million-dollar consulting jobs to survive."

But wait, PiedPiper—that sounds familiar. That sounds like where you work, Jason. But that must mean—

Yes, reader. I was one of the three engineers at SquidWorks who landed WarMonger as a client. Lightning does strike twice, and I would know because I can measure it with a frigging pocket-size weather station. Once our sister company became our main front, I took on the role of VP of operations and worked my way up to COO. That's ultimately because I put the success of the business first and because I got comfortable with being uncomfortable.

You can turn your asymmetry into an advantage, but you have to be risk-aware instead of risk-averse. (You cannot be comfortable being uncomfortable if you are risk-averse.) You've seen what an asymmetric advantage can offer a future, but don't get comfortable. It's time to get shit done.

CHAPTER 2

GET SHIT DONE

WHILE I WAS WORKING WITH SQUIDWORKS, I ALSO DID SOME FREELANCE work on the side as a free agent, and one of the clients I worked with was BombaWorks. At the time, they had Kickstarter funding and a lot of potential, but ultimately, all that boiled down to was an idea: they wanted to make a bike lock that enabled people to track their bikes and rent them out to other people.

Why did they need to hire a third-party consultant (aka me) before they could get shit done?

Two groups within BombaWorks were at war: one group was made of planners and perfectionists, while the other lived by the "move fast and break things" motto. The executive group, responsible for sales and account management, was selling promises and dreams; they'd hear out prospective clients' needs and then add those desires to their product's feature list. On Google and Facebook campuses, dozens of bikes were going missing every year, which cost the companies a lot of money, so the BombaWorks CEO (who was also head of sales, bless him) wanted to solve this problem.

The features list looked essentially like this:

- Let people rent the bikes through the lock directly; don't assume everyone has a smartphone!

- Okay, but of course, most people will have a smartphone, so go ahead and make an app that allows people to do this.

- Why did you make this app just for Android? iPhone users want to rent bikes too!

- Employees need to be able to scan their company badges on the locks to unlock them, for bikes on large campuses, so add a scanner somewhere next to the card swiper/vending-machine-style coin slot.

- Make sure the locks have GPS tracking capabilities. We can't stop thieves, but we can find them!

- Maybe an alarm could go off if a thief tries to take a campus-issued bicycle? Like a car alarm? But make sure they don't go off at the first sign of thunder; that's super annoying.

The executive group jotted down each prospect's needs, like Moses tabulating the Ten Commandments, and then they assigned the work to the two engineering groups. The software engineers saw the growing features list, and they were like, "Yeah, sure, we can do that." For them, it was just coding, then passing the features down the line. But at the other end of the line were the hardware engineers, the perfectionists in our story. The thing is, hardware engineering got its name for a reason: it's hard to do. While the software engineers were jumping these fences like trick ponies, the hardware team stood like elephants at the edge of each obstacle, dragging their feet.

Things got complicated when the executive team poached LinkedIn as a client: not only did LinkedIn want the bike locks, with their own myriad requests for the devices, but they also needed actual bicycles to put them on. But get this—pay attention because this will blow your mind—not all bikes are built the same way. So, the BombaWorks hardware team needed to either create multiple lock styles to fit the different types of bicycles or find a bike that would somehow fit all their future customer needs. LinkedIn wanted a trial run: twenty bikes with trackable locks in three months.

And the BombaWorks CEO, without consulting the hardware team, was like, "Sure, yeah, that seems perfectly reasonable." At which point the hardware team completely short-circuited and shut the hell down. No production was taking place at all.

The CEO and other pipe dreamers were growing increasingly impatient with the hardware team. Why couldn't they be more like their brother, software? It was clear they needed a company-family therapist to step in and serve as mediator here; otherwise, exactly zero shit was about to get done.

I kicked down BombaWorks's door, very professionally, and said, "Start taking features off the list. Stop assuming that people don't have smartphones. Forget about the alarms. We have to start somewhere and then build upon it while we can." They slowly started to peel those too-specific, conflicting feature ideas off of their list.

The twenty bicycles weren't quite feature-complete by the end of the three months, but they were 95 percent of the way there. The product was good enough to be in front of a customer.

The product wasn't perfect, but LinkedIn loved it: they loved that they knew precisely where their campus bicycles were stationed at the end of the day and which of their employees were being shady. It turned out that they didn't need all the bells and whistles that the BombaWorks CEO was trying to sell them.

So, the moral of the story here is: move fast, but maybe don't break *so many* things that the broken shards slow down your momentum.

What Shit Needs to Get Done?

Thanks to BombaWorks's example, we can see that getting shit done isn't just about self-discipline or time management or whatever else the usual business books tell you. It's a group effort, a constant balance between different personality types, wavering budgets, and areas of expertise. When it comes to your own company, consider: what is *the* thing that needs to get done *right now*? Then, get real and ask yourself, *Why hasn't it happened yet*? Bring clarity to the problem at hand. Let go of your destination, the ideal end product, while you're creating it. Sometimes you have to build something to see what you don't want it to be, then make it again.

Are you hung up on packaging? Stop. Are you waiting for your website to be beautiful before you launch the e-commerce portion of your business? Don't wait. Stop thinking about doing stuff and do it. Be willing to try and fail. Get comfortable being uncomfortable!

Have the discipline to stop the action long enough to take a step back and look at the big picture again. Have the discipline to switch gears as needed.

Let's look at some areas people try to inappropriately streamline. Then, we'll see why otherwise productive people aren't getting shit done and figure out how to fix that using asymmetric advantages.

BUILDING THE PRODUCT

BombaWorks's problem was taking a scattergun approach to building their product. They got so caught up in selling the dream, they forgot that it was something that actually needed to be built. Dreams are infinite, but real-life products—even technological ones—have their limits. The CEO and sales team weren't just talking to the big campuses at Facebook, Google, and Apple; they were also talking to *anybody* who was interested in a bicycle sharing program. If the focus had *just* been campuses, then they would have had a place to start, which is imperative when it comes to getting shit done. Lacking a specific starting point, everything began to get conflated into the product spec.

It would be tempting, as a small group of people who were agile and free from perfectionism, to say, "Let's go build a fighter jet and make some money," but you can't do it as a small group. SquidWorks could not have built a fighter jet. WarMonger is successful at building big projects because they have experts, money, a rigid corporate structure, tried and true processes, teams, and all of those kinds of things that we (small entrepreneurs) reject about the corporate world. They're good and valuable in that type of organization. Building a very complicated project and trying to overly simplify it to a small team leads you to this type of paralysis.

The BombaWorks guys were failing to finish because they lacked the ability to oscillate between the task and the big picture. Having the discipline every now and then to pull out and look at the big picture before diving back into the thing that you're doing is a very challenging skill. In a massive company, you never have to do that. There'll be someone at Apple who will only care about what shade of gold the gold iPhone is. They don't have to worry about the shape of the iPhone, or if it's even a phone; they just need to worry about a particular shade of a specific color.

To get shit done, you have to find a way to mediate between teams of people and different personality types. Getting shit done in a company, which is ultimately a team of people, boils down to communication from leadership to team members and between teams (if your team is big enough). That's why SquidWorks was able to win our Space Station client over WarMonger: WarMonger's teams weren't communicating with one another. We were just three guys, so communication abounded. The people who were working on the product were also the people who were talking to the client. That unique situation doesn't work at larger corporations, but it worked for us because we were able to understand, at least on a base level, the necessary work, who would fulfill which roles, the capabilities of the team, and—most importantly—how to motivate the team members to work harder than they (we) had ever done before.

You need the whole company to be all in on the plan to make that happen.

CONDUCTING MEETINGS

Google meetings start on time, and they finish five minutes before they finish. If you are in a meeting room at Google, people start knocking on the door at the top of the hour, so meetings do not run long at Google. Part of the reason that happened is that people were empowered to stop indulging conversation. It's not rude at Google to cut people off and say, "Let me stop you right there. We're out of time." Which sounds great! Very efficient. A well-oiled machine, as it were.

To the higher-ups at Google, blowing through another five minutes at the end of a meeting means you have no respect for anybody else's time. But if you look at that on the surface and you say, on day one of your company, "We're going to have every meeting start with an agenda, like at Amazon, and end every meeting on time, like Google," then you could be squashing some meandering meetings that could ultimately result in creative solutions to your business's unique problems.

If there are three or five or ten people at your little company, and you're all trying to solve this hard problem, it doesn't serve anyone to show up to a strictly timed meeting with a one-topic agenda. It's possible to reach a natural conclusion, but it might not happen until after you've had that conversation for the fifth time that week, and you've spent twenty hours talking about that topic because it's a *big* problem. You can't say, "Agenda item: let's name our company. We've got fifty-five minutes." No. To end up with something particularly good, you're going to set your heart on something and then realize that you can't use it because you can't get a domain name or a trademark or something like that. And that's going to take time. If you're copying Google and Amazon, then you won't give yourself the space you need to come up with the best name for *your* company.

People think they can just go and clone someone else's solution, but if your strategy is just "monkey see, monkey do," then you won't solve the problem for yourself.

STRETCHING YOUR DOLLAR

Money is a weird thing. Just in general. Depending on what you've done historically, you may not know how much you can do with how little money you might have. Many startups in technology germinate from college dorm rooms, and that can be an advantage because as a college student, you're pretty good at making money stretch. You don't have a lot of it, but you have desires to do stuff in the world or drink or eat or whatever it is. You have this forceful budget of having to earn money immediately to spend it on what you need. If you have less disposable income, you also have less time to dispose of it. You have more time to work stuff out or learn things or work on stuff.

Many times, you see startups blossom from Ivy League schools, kids who got high SAT scores, but there's no subsistence living going on in most of those institutions. There are very few kids that then have to go and get a job to have spending or Ramen-noodle-eating money. I don't want to make a gross generalization, but there is a level of comfort that comes from being at those types of places. It gives you the freedom to spend more time working on the thing that you're trying to work on. Zuckerberg could spend more time stealing other people's ideas for Facebook because he didn't have to slot that in with his shifts at Starbucks. Proof by obsidian.

There's another side to this: these kids start out with money as their advantage, but they never learned how to budget, which means they never learned how to stretch their dollar. They only know how to thrive, so survival isn't a skill they understand.

The same is true for people who come from big companies—places where there have been real budgets—and try to work at startups. They go, "What? I don't have a multi-million-dollar marketing budget? I can't possibly do any good marketing!" They either end up doing no marketing or getting their twelve-year-old kids to post some stuff on social media, both of which are terrible ideas. They should find an undergrad or the grad student who's trying to get some marketing experience and pay them to do the marketing. They're not going to be Saatchi & Saatchi, but they're also not going to cost Saatchi & Saatchi money. They're going to cost something commensurate with your startup needs.

Doing overly complicated financial modeling for startups is a waste of time. That's why this money thing is a challenging topic, but that's an advantage for you as a company when you don't have any money because you also don't need to spend a lot of time watching your money. You don't need a lot of accountants, financial controls, or purchasing rules because there's only a handful of people at your business, and you should all be able to work it out. You have more time to focus on the thing you're trying to build. The only thing that matters in this whole process is actually working on this thing that you're doing *every day*. You need enough money to get shit done, and make it work when you don't.

KNOWING ENOUGH TO GET STARTED

You have to know what you're trying to build, without necessarily knowing the end result. It's not even about the end result, which sometimes leads to paralysis in a business: people are inherently afraid of the unknown. *I can't write these product specifications because I can't verbalize or write down exactly what it is. I don't know exactly what I'm working toward.*

Maybe you have it worked out that you want to build an app like Instagram, an app that displays a square photo and shows up on a feed. There are a thousand decisions that went into Instagram before it became the successful platform that it is today, but first it started out as photo sharing. Now, I can like images, post ephemeral content, and write comments: all actions that grew organically from the idea of taking a photo and putting some filters on it. That's a fairly simple idea that's easy to execute and launch. Then, through testing or what have you, you can determine, "Actually, I want people to be able to teleport to these places in the pictures." That's quite a lot of work, but you know, dream big. Go for it. Just start somewhere. Just start.

The intangible part of getting shit done is knowing the answer to this question: does the world need this?

This is another bit you can't be taught at school.[2] There's a whole bunch of books that talk about this as a phenomenon, but it's about putting yourself in the right place. You have to be in touch with your intuition (your gut instinct) and then have the conviction to follow that intuition; that's what it really means to get comfortable being uncomfortable. People go to Silicon Valley because they're interested in changing the world; it's less about being *geographically* located somewhere than being in a particular state of mind. It's not even about changing the world as much as making an impact.

You should focus on changing the industry by bringing your invention or innovation to life. You generally see people come from two angles with that. One is the person who's been in the industry forever, who knows how completely broken it is and tries to fix it. Sometimes that works, and sometimes it becomes Quidditch, a fast-paced competition of computer

---

[2] Side rant: I always find it funny when people say they took courses in entrepreneurship because—isn't it a disqualifier for calling yourself an entrepreneur to go and do a course on entrepreneurship? You're supposed to build your business on your own. That's what sets entrepreneurs apart from other business people: they derive answers to solve problems that you can't find in a book.

wizardry, for people who come from an outsider perspective. That's the second angle: what you would consider the disruptors, the Ubers of the world. There were all of these town cars that chilled out between 10:00 a.m. and 4:00 p.m., until someone was like, "How about we put those drivers to work and then maybe we can just get anyone to be a driver?" Which is crazy. I still have not met anyone who can tell me the inherent difference between a taxi service and Uber, but Uber became synonymous and even superseded the taxi industry because it offered a different perspective.

It wasn't like someone who'd run the taxi companies went, "Well, there's a better way, sure." It was a guy who just wanted to tap a fake button on his touchscreen, not have to pay cash, and get to where he needed to go. There was a need there, and if you look, you'll see how that's applicable to other types of things. Uber Eats, for example, came a hell of a lot longer after Uber. If you look at the perfect model, you'd look at Uber today and go, "Wow, that's really clever! They do different types of rides, *and* they also deliver food, so that probably means that it's easy to get a ride. Sweet." But if you try to replicate that, you're going to get stuck at the drawing board. Your thing needs to solve a problem before it can take off.

DON'T TAKE YOUR ASYMMETRIC ADVANTAGE FOR GRANTED

BombaWorks's asymmetric advantage, even though they were a small team, was that they never had to struggle. They won TechCrunch Europe and had a Kickstarter that earned hundreds of thousands of dollars. All of those things sound amazing until you realize that they burdened the organization to such an extent that it became a self-fulfilling prophecy of needing to go and sell beyond their capabilities. They were money hungry, yet spent more and more money every month. They'd hired people who were successful and expensive when they could have purchased their "chairs" with a little more wear and tear and lower costs, if you know what I mean. It's hard to see that when you go, "Oh, but I'm one of twenty-five people on this small team. We have the asymmetric advantage," but that asymmetric advantage goes all the way down to the competitor, who's just one person in a shed doing what they're trying to do for next to nothing, in terms of cost. If they didn't maximize their asymmetric advantage by communicating with one another (because they had immediate access to one another), then they were never going to turn it into an advantage. Thankfully, they got their shit together and got shit done (in this chapter, at least).

Regardless of the specific role that you play organizationally, you have a role to play in not becoming paralyzed by perfectionism and moving fast enough to wind your competitors without breaking too many things. That's the secret: move fast but don't break so much that you can't recover in the long term. You can't clone what someone else did and make it work for you.

GET SHIT DONE AT YOUR OWN STARTUP

The hiccup at BombaWorks was something that often happens in an early-stage company: the sales team, particularly the

CEO, was selling hopes and promises. He was selling whatever sounded good. His *intentions* were admirable. He thought, *I've got a great team. These guys can do anything. I'm just going to go and sell whatever I can get away with selling, and basically, we'll work it out.* Which is 100 percent the right thing to do; that behavior should not be discouraged in any way, shape, or form. In my opinion, if you can technically do it, you should go sell the dream, because the dream is more attainable to *your* tech-related startup than other types of startups. You have engineers and developers working for you: they're the closest things to wizards that exist. The trick to remember is that working in technology is magical, yes, but it isn't quite magic. It's close, but you have to remember the human limitations to the process and, therefore, to the dream you're selling. As long as you have that in mind, absolutely go off and work out how to sell the thing that you have or the thing you nearly have.

The startup mantra of "move fast and break things" exists for a reason. It can be horribly uncomfortable for some—or even for most. In many instances, it can work well; in others, it can sink the company. When you can find the balance, that's when the magic starts to happen. You can't successfully run a company unless you learn how to get shit done.

If you have a smaller team like SquidWorks and BombaWorks, then you actually have an advantage: when the giants are sleeping on the weekends, you can be hustling and taking their customers. But you have to understand the myth of work-life balance and methods for dealing with the pressure.

CHAPTER 3

BALANCE AND PRESSURE

MY FRIEND GABRIEL INVITED ME TO SPEND A WEEK ON A PRIVATE YACHT— owned by the guy who started Google Maps—in Greece for free a while back, and I, of course, said, "Hell yeah, I'm already packing," but there was just one problem: we were launching a new product at PiedPiper that same week.

Our CEO at the time was acting like this product was going to be the next iPhone. We were still a relatively small company back then, so all hands were on deck. I couldn't just tell my team, "See ya in a week!" and then disappear in a series of snorkeling sounds. But there was no way in hell I was going to pass up the opportunity to rub elbows with up-and-coming leaders in tech—on a freaking boat—in another freaking country.

I didn't exactly have the budget to say, "No, thanks, mate; I'll pay my own way to float around the Greek islands next week when I'm free."

So, I decided to do both.

I told my team that I'd be working remotely on the product launch, and that was true. I worked California hours in Europe, which was a doozy, but I got to be on a YACHT. For FREE. In GREECE. This was not a work-cation; I wasn't just checking my emails occasionally while I was away, putting out fires as needed. I was wor-*king*.

Don't worry about me, though: the energy on the yacht was excellent. Everyone was so grateful to be there. It was like being on this guilty-pleasure show I watch on Bravo called *Below Deck*. If you haven't seen the show, don't bother. You will not get any smarter from watching it. It's horrible. But it's also horribly great, and being on the yacht, metaphorically on the set, made my *life* horribly great by extension.

Work and Vacation Like the Rich—Even If You Aren't

People don't start companies because they want an easy life. They start them because they're trying to take on an entire industry. When your goal is this large, you don't have time to vacation in the traditional sense, sorry to tell you.

I'm not trying to say there's no such thing as work-life balance. I'm saying work-life balance is just called "life."

You have to find small ways to balance the pressure in your life. Working odd hours in Greece is how I managed to do it during PiedPiper's major product launch, and traveling is a key option here, but avoiding burnout and honoring monk time are some other ways to go about it.

GET THE HELL OUT OF THE OFFICE

It's amazing how little relief an honest-to-God vacation can bring you. A new experience or a new place just acts as a slight pressure relief valve, but the knob on your Stress Dial just moves from Fully Fucking Overwhelmed down to Still Overwhelmed Because I'm Still Thinking about Work. I'm not saying *don't* take a vacation. If you can do that, then for sure do. But changing up your views (physically and metaphysically) on a *daily* basis can be a great way to balance the demands and decrease the pressure of running a startup.

Your mindset changes, your anxiety goes down a notch, if you go and get some fresh air—get away from your desk for a few minutes, a few hours, walk off, walk away from your agenda (as a line item in your agenda). Now, more than ever, burnout is so rampant with everyone working from home during the pandemic. There's no distinction between work life and home life because it's all happening in the same location. My dining table has become my workstation, and that's true for a lot of other people too.

South of San Francisco, where I live and work, I can go to a little place by the beach for two hours, and for me, that offers some pressure relief. Take the opportunity to walk down a different street or even just around the place that you live. Have the mindset of like, "Hey, let's walk down the street and see if there's anything new," and then the next thing you know, you're stumbling into a new café you never noticed before, and voila, you have a new place to get work done. A place with a new view.

This crazy startup life of long hours and not a lot of sleep and a lot of stress can kill you if you're not careful. When you're trying to do things that you genuinely believe are going to change an industry or the world, you forget to change things up. You forget to look up from your work.

When you can take a second, then, take micro-vacations, if you like. Go see something beautiful for a second; travel to another place and work from home like I did in Greece. It's totally attainable for those of us in this line of business.

There aren't a lot of techy startups where people are looking at the clock at 9:00 a.m. to make sure everyone's at their desk on time. It's always going to be, by its nature, a pretty fluid work environment. It's more about creating your deliverables and meeting your deadlines than the actual hours of bum-in-chair.

Take one of the guys who works with us and lives in the UK, as an example. He works with people on a daily basis in the US as well as the UK. He also has two daughters under three, and so he has structured his life, for the most part, such that he wakes up early to attend to his children, and then gets everyone on their way and works for a couple of hours. Once he knows everyone's good and no one needs him, he can chill out in the afternoon. He spends that time with his wife and his kids. He makes time to see his dad, who's getting older. Then, he gets back online after dinnertime and stays virtually available until nine thirty, ten o'clock at night. It's that little break in the middle of the day—that micro-vacation—to which he attributes being able to do his job without keeling over from a stress-induced heart attack. He's in a VP role, so that's pretty stressful; lots of good and bad things happen on a regular basis.

To him, these moments with his family are more important than going on a ten-day vacation in Singapore or where have you. He's structured his schedule in a way that even if he has a god-awful start to his day, he gets this four- to five-hour break where people are not expecting him to be online. He's able to fulfill his personal wants and needs as the husband; he can also do work.

In a small startup, especially in the early days, work can be all day every day. The Monday-through-Friday workweek is for people who are fine with the status quo, but for world-changers like us, we need to stay busy. We need to strike while our competition is resting. We have to find a way to keep going. These micro-vacations can help you achieve that and avoid burnout.

AVOID BURNOUT BY HOLDING BOUNDARIES

Humans, in general, are not malicious creatures. We're not walking around trying to fuck with each other.[3] There are some exceptions, but generally, we're not gazelles in the savanna, trying to live our lives when suddenly a giant goddamn cat attacks us.

When people do not respect your time or energy, you have to realize it's because there is a deficiency in your behavior: You answer the phone at all hours. If a friend calls and you haven't spoken to them in a long time and you're feeling guilty about that, then you may let them take up hours of your time,

---

[3] If you think that people are actively out to get you, it's vital to investigate your past traumas to understand where this feeling is coming from.

even if you don't have the energy for it. You say yes to projects you don't have time for because you're addicted to being praised for your hard work.

All of these behaviors lead to burnout—but people only get burnt out because they haven't set boundaries.

If you're used to getting positive feedback when you work on something, then saying no means you're not getting that affirmation, and that might leave you feeling useless. Instead of saying no, then, say, "Not right now." Let them know that you're busy by briefly explaining what you're working on and what your schedule looks like, but also let the requester know that their concerns/feedback/time is important to you, so they're not feeling dismissed. Setting boundaries also means setting expectations.

If you genuinely feel in charge of yourself and your own schedule, you're not going to feel partial to each coworker's whim.

Protecting yourself from burnout helps guard your organization against failure. You're a leader at your startup agency. Your role is essential. Make sure you're available for your team when they really, truly need you.

Setting boundaries took me a long time to get down; I had to actively work on the process with coaches and mentors. It'll be hard work, but nailing the art of healthy boundary-setting will enable you to balance the pressure of your life. The boundaries apply to your whole life, not work alone.

My mother is basically retired, so when she gets me on the phone, she's got days to talk. Not to say that she has nothing to do, but her time is generally more flexible, whereas I might have a thirty-minute window open. With my mindset today, I can remind myself that I'm *choosing* to use that thirty minutes to call my mother, so now, I let her know upfront that I only have that much time to be on the phone. "Okay," she says, completely nonplussed. "Perfect." Boom: the expectation has been set. I don't need to sit there and look at the clock going, "Oh God, I have to wrap this conversation up and get her to stop talking in five minutes because I need to get onto the next phone call."

If you're the kind of person whose identity is, "I answer every Slack message, I answer every email, I answer every text message, and I'm getting all of my work done," then you need to make some adjustments. That work ethic is just not sustainable. You need to get comfortable with being uncomfortable and reassess your professional identity.

MONK TIME

These wonderful devices that keep us connected during quarantine also technically make us available 24/7. If you succumb to all the notifications, answering every single one that comes in, then burnout lies on your horizon. You don't have to have a doctorate in psychology to see that. No part of that is healthy.

You can approach this problem in two ways: one, you can go, "I'm going to be a complete Luddite, and I'm just going to run around with a flip phone, like, 'What's this email thing? Send me a fax,'" which is not very 2021; or two, you have to work out how to set digital boundaries for yourself.

My chief of staff and I spend a lot of time chatting about the events of the workday. She'll say, "Hey, this person's having this problem, and this person's having that problem. What can we do? What training can we do for people?" That became too much to deal with on a daily basis with both of our screens constantly lighting up with new messages from people. To make things more manageable, we came up with this notion that we call "monk time," which is a period of my calendar that gets blocked out so I can go completely offline. I generally try and do things *not* on my computer, and I turn my phone off. It's a daily digital detox, in a way, but it helps you achieve a few screen-free line items in your to-do list. I use this time to come up for air and look at the big picture. I ask myself questions like, "Am I putting assets in the right places? Should I be focusing on something else? Have I lost sight of the big picture because I've been so focused on a crisis at hand?" I usually block off around four hours of monk time in my day.

Now, sometimes, I *have* to use technology for something strategic, so then I allow myself to use my laptop, because I'm not necessarily going to sit there and handwrite a bunch of notes to then have to create again digitally. If I cheat during monk time, I'll generally use a very plain text editor that I can put into no-distraction mode, and that can be my scratch pad. If I open Google Docs and then I get a notification that I've been tagged in some document, it's hard to stay undistracted, especially as someone who's got a lot going on and doesn't have an Adderall prescription.

I don't always work during monk time, though. Here's what I'm allowed to do in that period of time: unwind; take a nap; go for a walk; do something I *want* to do. If you're thinking, "You can do that on the weekends!"—ha ha, nice try. Weekends look a lot like the rest of my week, and if you're leading a startup, then that's likely how it is for you too.

Getting off technology is hard to do when you're a technologist and moving in a technological world. You might feel a bit like an addict at first: you get the shakes, putting the phone down like, "Oh God, what's going to happen in the next two hours? I can't do this!"

I know it's hard. Just think of it as time out, not time off. There almost isn't time off because it's all go, go, go. But in that little period of time when you can check out, you don't have to be online, so you don't have to deal with a crisis. Very rarely, the things that appear to be crises are actual crises. It's all relative. And you'll find that crises simply don't appear as often when you stay on top of your boundaries. If you don't have strong boundaries, then it's all, "My God, the sky is falling! It's all over! We're done for!" If you let the small stuff become a crisis, guess what? It's all small stuff. Therefore, everything becomes a crisis. So, take your monk time while you can get it.

Jason, Are You Sure It'll Be Okay?

Listen. Yes, I'm sure. It really is okay for you to step away. It's okay to tell your team members, no, and it's okay to be off your phone during the day and take a walk during business hours and even work remotely from another country. The company won't burn down in the meantime. Most likely.

Here's how I know: during this week when I was busting my ass and living my best life in Greece with my friend Gabriel, the new product launched at PiedPiper.

It was the first direct-to-consumer (DTC) product that we got all the way to the end. We started with a blank sheet of paper, and we ended up with this beautiful glossy white box. It was being presented as part of a keynote at a fairly large conference, and the CEO at the time had a whole bunch of press planned for it. There was a website launch.

Something that big in your company is likely to be one of the most horrible weeks of your life; we didn't have the leniency to mess it up, but something was destined to go wrong. We knew that. We knew that there were any number of outcomes. A product launch is a super vulnerable point for a newer company. Launching a product rolls you over and opens you up to public criticism and abject failure.

Even big companies do product launches, and they're often duds. No one's texting from their Fire Phones, for example; the only fire involved was how badly that thing crashed and burned. That's embarrassing. When you're at a small new company, though, you really need that thing to work. It's a pretty stressful time all around, and you also don't have the luxury of just throwing money at the problem, which obviously a big company does.

At PiedPiper, we wanted to make sure that we had a web store so that people could actually buy these products from us. We had glamour shots of the product that we put into the keynote presentation. We were trying to write press releases to attract the right type of press.

Was it the next iPhone? Hardly. We definitely overshot our expectations, but you couldn't say we under-delivered. The product launch was successful, generating seven figures of revenue, which kept the company alive. It was the main reason that the company was able to raise the next round of financing.

Mission accomplished. I got to have my yacht and eat tzatziki too.[4]

Balance the Pressure

Working hard should not equate to some "I don't sleep, and I work all the time" tech-bro flex. We all know we need to work hard, but we also need to take time to rest. The fastest way to crash your laptop is to keep it running, day and night, and the same is true for humans.

Balancing pressure, as a tool, is not "work hard, play hard" in the traditional sense. It's about finding a way to love what you do, so it doesn't feel like work. If traveling and working simultaneously does that for you, then great. As a tech startup leader yourself, you will have the luxury of traveling, but you should also consider everyday ways to recharge and avoid burnout.

In other words, your asymmetric advantage, when working at a tech-related startup, is your ability to unwind, which

---

4 One of the guys on the boat with us was completely obsessed with tzatziki. I don't know if it was a preexisting condition or if he developed it on the trip, but at every stop we made, he would go to a restaurant and order tzatziki—a pint of it—to go. It became this inside joke that we (those of us who were not this one guy) were never going to get tzatziki ever again once we got home. There was a surplus of tzatziki on the boat at one point. Just too much tzatziki. So much of it.

enables you to maintain the stamina to lead your company, your designated branch, and your employees—which can also be a huge help in maintaining the culture you're trying to cultivate at your business.

CHAPTER 4

CULTURE

I CONSULTED FOR A COMPANY BASED IN GERMANY THAT HAD FRIDAY meetings that were weekly debrief/happy hour hybrids. Their higher-ups thought these meetings made them the king of culture. Who doesn't love an excuse to have a few drinks, especially when they're free? They wanted to keep everyone in the loop and have fun doing it—what's so wrong with that? Because different people spoke and gave presentations at these meetings, more people received visibility in the company; departments got to hear from others that they didn't interact with regularly, so the range of connection wasn't so siloed.

Then, the company expanded to California. They wanted to keep up the weekly tradition and encourage involvement from the different locations. New workers were being asked to give presentations, with just a few days to prepare. People began to dread and even fear being selected to give their oral pop quiz. But it was the time zones that were the real killer: when it was 5:00 p.m. on a Friday in Germany—a perfectly appropriate time to have a beer—it was 9:00 a.m. on Friday in California. Again, this was a German company, so alcohol consumption was reasonably prominent, and things are more relaxed at tech agencies than corporate businesses, but even our industry frowns upon getting a buzz on at the *start* of the workday.

The worst part about these fun-while-you-work meetings was that they were mandatory. People had no choice but to attend, even if it didn't fit with their schedule, even when the CEO no-call-no-showed to the meeting himself.[5]

People just stopped showing up to the meeting, almost like a boycott, sneakily Slacking their work BFFs, "If the CEO's not going to show up, then why should I?" The people who were involved were never empowered to own the meeting. It was the CEO's meeting, so it was a lot of pressure on everyone.

Cue the deep-voiced narrator of our sitcom: *it turns out, the mandatory meetings were not fun.*

I was the consultant for this company, yes, but I wasn't hired to share my professional opinion about this particular issue. I gave it, but it wasn't well received. To absolve my involvement in this poor "culture" choice, I'd like to say: I told them they should just take the meetings the way of Quibi and let it die. They should call it a "happy hour" or an "all hands," where a smaller group of people could provide an update. It should be held every other week or maybe even once a month.

And now that their company has tanked, I'd like to say, professionally and cordially: I told you so.

---

[5] Because he was off surfing in Hawaii, not because he was on a business trip or anything.

What's So Wrong with a Mandatory Party?

I would go so far as to say the culture of the German/Californian company (purposefully anonymous) was absolutely a factor in their demise. This culture of forced connection contributed to the poor attitude of the company overall. The thing is, the toxicity didn't sprout up overnight. There were so many warning signs: procrastination, lack of participation, lack of enthusiasm, to name a few. Like a knife fight in a phone booth, you want to dodge as many things going wrong as possible, and instead, these guys were making a collect call in slow motion.[6]

We know that, in business, something is absolutely bound to go wrong every now and then: you release a product that doesn't work, someone drags you on Reddit, or the CEO forgets to post his OOO before a company-wide meeting, once. But bad culture, a systemic issue, doesn't have to be one of them.

These days, Friday night happy hour is less frequent, as fewer people drink for a myriad of reasons. In other words, it's not as likely for startups to use alcohol as an elixir for awkward social gatherings. But there is still this global idea that extracurricular interaction between employees should take place at least occasionally, and we can blame at least part of that myth on the big-tech companies.

---

6 Younger readers, just ask Alexa what a "collect call" is if you're curious, but rest assured, it requires quite a bit of ham-fingered button-pushing, so they'd be bacon in this hypothetical knife fight.

The Big-Tech Lessons on Culture

The CEO at this German/Californian company woke up one day and thought, *I read half an article one time, and it says that if you want your team to bond, you should do a retro thing. Let's do that too. Let them drink beer. Fuck it.* They tried to replicate the public processes of all the unicorn companies, like Netflix and Google. No one was actually thinking about how the culture was going to come together.

I remember a very early meeting that I had with someone at Google, and they told me about how the powers that be liked it there. "Oh, it's so amazing," they said. "You can send an email to your boss at 3:00 a.m., and he'll reply."

That thinking's not amazing at all—it's disgusting.

The higher-ups at Google manage productivities and understand where the most efficacy of the teams resides. It's not just Google; all big-tech companies do this right now. It comes full circle back into the reason why LinkedIn was interested in BombaWorks and being able to track their bicycles: they spent millions of dollars doing analysis on the most effective and efficient way for people to move between buildings on a big campus, and the answer is a bicycle.

That seems cool on the surface. This big-tech company has all these multicolored fancy bikes. Well, the only reason they have these bikes is because they worked out that if their employees walk from one building to another to get to a meeting, they stop at Starbucks and grab a coffee and show up five minutes late. If they drive, they have to find parking, and that's dead time. They decided to "let" everyone ride skateboards and bicycles around campus, so they seem like the fun, hip place to work, but really, it's just that their research was right. Bicycles are more efficient.

Consider the benefits at these places and investigate them. Why do you get things like free on-site laundry if you work at a big-tech company? It's because if you get free laundry, you'll probably stay on campus to do your laundry and work longer.

It's insidious all the way down to the bus schedules. There'll be a bus at 4:30 p.m., and there'll be a bus at 5:30 p.m., but you can't get your company-funded dinner until after 5:00 p.m. If you want to stay for the free meal, they automatically get somewhere between thirty to forty-five minutes more work out of you because you don't really have anywhere to go between 4:30 p.m. and 5:00 p.m.

Toxic Cultures

My exposure to the tech cultures comes from a close friend who works in operations at Facebook. I know a lot of what happens in there. A big company is only going to talk about something that's self-serving because they have shareholders and a stock price. Facebook's not going to come out and go, "Oh my God, we have a really toxic work culture! And we solved it all by having retros on a Friday afternoon!" They're only ever going to talk about it when something bad happens, like what happened at Uber, where they *had* to talk about there being a toxic work culture.

There were so many people who were being sexually harassed, and it was going to end up on the front page of the *New York Times* one way or another. All good PR people will tell you to own the narrative. "If you tell the story, you own the narrative. If someone else tells the story, *stay on* the narrative." And that's exactly what big companies do, which makes sense. If I was the CEO of Uber, I would have gotten right out in front of the issue and said, "Yes, we know, but we're fixing it. And this is *how* we're fixing it." But either way, it's unlikely that if you ask people inside Uber genuinely, "Did they fix it?" that they'll say, "Yes." But the real answer is they shouldn't have ever had to. They let their culture get out of control.

Going and replicating the "fun" cultures of big-tech companies may seem like a good idea because they look really cool, but trust me, it's a mistake. Once you investigate the heart of the alleged benefit of that culture, then you can see the toxicity at its roots. You cannot spot the toxicity in your own culture by inspecting another, though. You have to fluctuate between big- and small-picture views. You have to get comfortable being uncomfortable to zoom in and out like this to keep your business in check.

You Can't Pay People to Care

Many startup leaders, in their early days at least, believe they can only afford to pay entry-level rates.[7] The benefits aren't great either—no retirement plan, disability insurance, or maternity leave. So, startup leaders usually try to make up for what they lack with a "fun culture," which usually translates

---

7 This is a myth that comes with the pressure to expand team size, but we'll cover this more in the next chapter.

to Ping-Pong tables in the break room and a policy that looks the other way if teammates drink after 2:00 p.m.

With this mindset comes low-toned gossip around the office Keurig: these fresh-out-of-college employees have figured out that "living to work" is a scam, so they're just trying to "work to live," and they have a growing resentment toward the company. They thought things would be different, that they could afford to travel and pay their rent at the same time. Maybe they looked up the salary range for entry-level positions on Glassdoor, and they're feeling pretty cheated. Just as the team members stopped showing up to the Friday meetings at the German/Californian company, so too in these cases, we see a kind of toxic stalemate. "If they wanted good work out of us," the employees say, "they'd pay us more."

It's over at this point, from one startup leader to another. You can't pay people to care if they don't care. Pizza parties and Ping-Pong tables may be an extrinsic part of the paycheck, done to energize the employees. You want them to feel like it's fun to come to work—but no number of perks or salary increases will make someone think it's fun to work on something they're not passionate about.

Especially in the early stages of your company, you need people to care. You need people to share your vision, to see it clearly the way you do, so that the dream can become a reality. Without contagious passion for the work and all hands on deck, your company isn't going to get off the ground. It's not going to get its fair chance to change the world.

At this point, when you've caught wind of the office gossip (a sure sign of a toxic culture), you can squash it in one of two ways: one, you can try to find work that motivates your disgruntled team members, or two, you can let them go. We'll cover how to know when it's time to let go in the next section.

The most mundane tasks to you could be soothing to others. Don't assume that your tedious tasks are going to scare off your newer team members. It's important to delegate, and sometimes, just cluing the team members in on how they're helping you out can make them feel like their work has a sense of purpose. Work doesn't have to be "fun" necessarily; it just has to make people feel like they're working toward something important. If they see your vision, then taking tasks off of your plate can be meaningful.

If your team members feel disenchanted with their work, even when you know for sure they share your vision, then it might be that the team member is in the wrong role. Sit them down in your next one-on-one and investigate their true interests. If they're in sales, maybe they want to work in production. That's a tricky one: you want people who can operate with excellence on your product because you're trying to make something amazing, not something a novice could make. But if you can make this team member feel involved with the work in some way to reignite their passion, then changing their position can go a long way.

More than anything, it's important to remember that you don't have to make affordances or excuses for people just because you're a startup. It's not a disadvantage that you can't pay Facebook and Google salaries or offer Netflix cultural benefits. You just have to reimagine your situation and find your asymmetric advantage. You have more to offer than you're giving yourself credit for.

When employees don't care about your vision, that means they're just showing up for a paycheck, from a finite pool of money your company has. Every penny counts in the early days of your business, so for them to take all that money and not care, well, you're better off just getting rid of them.

This is something in the Netflix culture deck that's out there on the internet: at the end of month, they sit team members down and say, "If we give you three thousand bucks, will you leave?" This helps them weed out the people who are passionate about the work from the people who are just there for a paycheck. Obviously, at a startup, you don't have any money to be throwing away like this; that's kind of the whole point of this section. Even the big-tech companies who seem to have money to throw away can't afford to pay uninspired employees. You should be thinking about this too.

When It's Time to Let Go

Note: this section is about your original team members, the people who were behind the idea since the beginning, but who haven't pulled their weight. In the next chapter, I talk more about hiring on the right people, which can absolutely impact culture for the better (or worse, if you're not intentional about it).

I don't expect everyone to work a hundred-hour week and engineer themselves to death—quite the opposite. I'm happy if my team members work hard for two hours, deliver exceptional work, and then do nothing else. You can see signs that someone is simply signing the attendance sheet and showing up to get their paycheck.

It's not because they're busy with something else in their life. If they were planning their wedding, having a child, or taking on some large external thing, they might be distracted but not checked out, and they would probably talk about that exciting other thing that's going on in their life.

The checked-out employee spends their time either thinking about something else or working on something else—on your dime—and as a startup, you can't afford to have checked out employees.

Before letting them go, investigate why they're checked out. Do they not care about their work, or are they overwhelmed? Maybe they don't really understand what you've asked them to do, either in a specific task or in a new role. They could be failing, not because they aren't trying, but because they fundamentally don't understand what's going on.

You could offer to move them to a different position, and it won't necessarily make any difference to them. For example, you could say to them, "Hey, you've expressed interest in [XYZ title and responsibilities]. Is that something you like doing then?" Then, they'd look at you under hooded eyes and say, "Like, maybe. Yeah." But when you give them an opportunity, they literally don't do anything with it. And, if they just wanted a new job title, and they don't actually do the work, then you have to ask yourself, "Is this someone that I want to invest in?"

There are two ways of knowing when you need to let go, and those two things are not mutually exclusive. My work at

SquidWorks has given me a lot of experience with working with the military, so here's another war metaphor for you: ultimately, we have an army run by generals, but it would work as well as an army run by privates. One is quite a bit more expensive than the other.

The general's not thinking about whether there's enough rounds of ammunition in his backpack versus what's going to happen in two months' time. He's thinking big picture. The private is thinking about whether or not he's going to wake up tomorrow, not what's going to happen in two months' time. But I think there is a point where people also hate their natural levels. Maybe the private *wants* to start thinking more big picture, even if he's not in the right headspace to do that effectively.

I'm a big advocate for giving everyone second chances, but to give second chances, you have to bring up these tough topics early with your team members. You have to set expectations and give them time to improve.

I see a lot of this in companies: there's a CEO who's been the dominant leader in an organization, meaning that they do a lot of hand-holding, but then you get to a place where that's no longer possible because the leader is thinking about things at a much higher level than the individual contributors. At that point, you have to start bringing in middle management and implementing new team strategies.

But there's no startup pack that you get as a small company that says, "Okay, you've now got fifty-three people, and you've done half a million dollars in sales. It's time to initiate Plan B."

It's tough. I get it. That's why it's important to be comfortable with being uncomfortable, so you can keep the presence of mind to evaluate the possible failings in your company. If you hired the wrong people, then the culture can easily get toxic. To protect your culture—to ensure the success of your business—you need to let these people go. We'll cover how to find the right people for your startup in the next chapter.

How to Cultivate a Culture of Camaraderie

You can intentionally create culture, but camaraderie has to happen organically. It can grow more easily in a company with ten people, who have in-office happy hours during work hours, where people are allowed to have fun—but if they need to get their work done, they can without being alienated for it. Camaraderie is seeing someone working hard and asking them, "Hey, can I bring you a beer back to your desk?" or "Would you like a snack? or "Hey, when you get to a stopping point, why don't you come and join us?"

Saying, "Everyone, at four o'clock get off your desk. You have to go into this meeting room, and you have to sit down and then—one, two, three: have fun!" won't build a positive culture. But startup leaders tend to think like that.

I've literally been to companies, seen their "culture," and thought, with all the compassion in my heart, "Wow, you really thought that was going to work. You're dumber than I thought you were."

But I get it; I understand the appeal of trying to manufacture connection in a company. When your schedule is that busy, you feel like you need to schedule the fun; otherwise, when will you have it? That's why it's so important to master balance and pressure before we get to this point in a company. And when I say "master," I want you to realize I don't mean that it's a destination you arrive at and then that's it. Just like everything else, it's something you have to work at. It requires a constant fluctuation between being present-minded and forward-thinking, and that shift in attention is uncomfortable. You have to be comfortable in that uncertainty.

This is analogous to a military boot camp. The boot camp performs three functions:

- to offer basic training,

- to weed out those who are there for the wrong reason, and

- to build camaraderie during times of adversity or hardship.

It's the same with something like BUD/S, the US Navy SEAL course. You can't force the camaraderie, but you can create an environment for it to flourish. Startups can often be places of real adversity…but clearly they shouldn't be run like boot camps!

The point is: don't schedule fun for later. Find a way to have fun right now, and teach your team members how to do the same.

In the early days at PiedPiper, we had ten to twenty people working all around the world. (We're a mostly remote company.) Once a year, we wanted everyone to see each other in person, so we could all feel like a real team, not just voices on the computer. We scraped together enough money to put people up in hotels in San Francisco, near our headquarters, but after that, we didn't really have the funds to feed people, let alone take them out on the town. But we wanted to do something fun; we wanted to create an atmosphere that could inspire connection.

I'm an okay cook. I'm no Gordon Ramsay, but I do okay. With the help of one of the other leaders, I hosted a barbecue cookout, so we could gather all the team members in one place and feed them at the same time.

Everyone loved it. It felt familial and gave everyone the impression that this was for fun *only*; it wasn't meant to spice up the work they needed to do back at their desks necessarily. Of course, that was at the heart of it, but the interactions were genuine, starting from the leadership and spreading throughout the team base. It created a culture of camaraderie at PiedPiper.

Now, we have over fifty team members, and we have the funds to pay for hotel rooms *and* fancy dinners. But we still host the barbecues. We need quite a few more cooks to feed this many people, but the OG crew, the Day One team members, loved the cookouts, and we put in the work to keep the tradition alive.

You don't need a bunch of money to cultivate an inspiring, welcoming culture. You just need authenticity and openness.

Turning a Friday-Meeting Culture Around

"Well, that's all fine and good," you're probably saying, "but what if you already have a toxic, big-tech-company-copying culture?"

Let's go back to the German/Californian company example: the happy-hour all-hands monstrosity had metastasized throughout their culture, so they took something positive and ruined it by morphing it into something that it wasn't ever meant to be, without thinking about what they were trying to do. No one really owned the Friday meetings. They just tried to clone from a concept that existed inside a different, larger, more successful organization and slap their own badge on it.

There are two things they could have done to heal their toxic culture: One, they could have killed the Friday retros, and they could have just said, "Look, the retro isn't really a retro. Let's call it what it is: a happy hour." Two, they could have had a *separate* meeting as an all-hands, so different teams had the floor to provide an update. This meeting could have occurred during a time that was convenient for people on both sides of the world and taken place every other week or once a month. Really, just utilize Google Hangouts and have the head of software talk about software and the head of hardware talk about hardware and so on.

At PiedPiper, we've learned that having a mostly remote company doesn't hurt the culture at all. People think it's a disadvantage to not have a single office building to house your employees, but it actually provides an opportunity to form a different type of culture. Plus, once you realize you are a remote company, then you have a wider pool from which to fish out exceptional recruits.

PiedPiper employees are called "Pipers." Instead of having a single virtual happy hour (which would be difficult since our team is located all around the world), we have two "Piper Sessions": one on a California morning for the international folks, then one at the end of the California day, so we company leaders can meet with everyone in the US. Before we host a Piper Session, about once every six weeks, we premake a fifteen-minute video to educate the team about what's going on in the company. We call this "Piper TV," and it's "aired" a few days before the Piper Session, so people can ask the CEO or other C-suite members questions at the start of the actual Session. It's like a Reddit AMA for the CEO, basically. We also have a Slack channel called #thewatercooler, where we can all get together and talk about things that specifically do not pertain to work, like beekeeping.[8]

Anyway, that sounds like a seemingly oversimplified solution—easier said than done—and that's true. It is somewhat reductionist to think, *just stop doing the toxic thing and your company won't be toxic.* But it can be that simple, as long as you're willing to put in the hard work. You have to stay aware and regularly check on the health of the product as well as the health of your team *and* individual team members. This will ensure the success of your culture and your company. Remember: you can absolutely have a remote team and have a culture. Location is not greater than or equal to culture at all.

---

[8] True story: one #thewatercooler chat session was dedicated to our surprisingly shared love of bees. The office was abuzz with connection.

Cultivate Culture—Not Culture Shock

Culture is something that you create. It's this sacred thing that you don't want to lose. But there's also bad culture, something that creeps up unintentionally, so sometimes culture is something you need to *re*-create.

Culture doesn't become a noun until you've got lots of people, but it does exist from Day One. Everyone thinks culture means happy employees or swag or everyone being on Slack, but it's actually everything: the processes, the attitudes, the work itself. It's the people. Do people feel like they can pick up the phone and call anyone they need to if they're in a crisis at your company? The answer to that question says a lot about your company atmosphere.

Cultivate a culture where connections can happen organically; don't try to force closeness with mandatory meetings and team-building exercises. Understand the difference between what is valuable to your company and what is valuable to your team members.

And understand this: you can't scale culture. There's no scaling the business and going, "Wow, we're amazing. We've built a business with a hundred people, so now we have culture." You have to make sure you have a solid culture among your OG team members before you start introducing new people into the mix. From there, it's important to identify if/when things go wrong with your culture, so you can course correct.

CHAPTER 5

SCALING

AT PIEDPIPER, WE PROMOTED ONE OF THE SALES TEAM MEMBERS TO VP of sales, and we figured out quickly that they weren't capable of fulfilling their new responsibilities. He wasn't actually doing any of the things that you would want out of someone who's leading a team at that level. He was just there because our investors wanted someone in the org chart who had that job title on the website and someone who would report sales figures at a board meeting.

When the CEO left, I inherited the sales team. The sales team had been operating for three or four months while we were mitigating the disaster that the former CEO had left us. I had to sit down with the poor, unqualified VP of sales, and he knew what was coming. He said, "I didn't really know that I needed to do reporting and managing the team and *still* be doing my sales job."

I had to have a hard conversation with him and say, "I'm going to have to change your job title because it's just not working out. We're going to flatten out the team."

Being demoted is a very demoralizing thing to happen to anybody. When he was promoted, it was a big thing, and he was very proud of the fact that this was the first time that he'd been a VP. He had a son who was a senior in high school, and those are all very positive messages to a child: you work hard; you get promoted; you get recognition. How humiliating to celebrate that promotion with your family and teach your children the lesson of the American Dream on a local scale, just to go home and have your spouse go, "How was your day, honey?"

"Yeah, it was terrific. I got demoted."

Now, he has to go on LinkedIn and change his job title. That's a horrible reality. And it was just completely unnecessary to have had to do that process and cause that trauma. All because we made an unnecessary decision to satisfy an external influence's desire to tick a box that said "VP of sales." These are people we're working with, not numbers to crunch or boxes to check off.

Stand Up for Your (True) Needs

Companies sometimes feel an external pressure to expand. That itch to grow can be put onto your plate by investors or a board of directors because they're more concerned with filling the org chart than fulfilling an organizational need.

If an investor says, "Well, you should really think about getting an executive assistant," the dumb answer is to go and find an executive assistant. The smart answer is to work out what you actually need—which may require you to do the really horrifying, palm-sweating, pants-wetting task of telling the investors, "You're wrong." But you don't say it like that. Say, "Actually, I've done some research and determined that I don't need an executive assistant. What I need is someone who can do XYZ things or prioritize organization in my weekly tasks, and So-and-so has agreed to fulfill those responsibilities for a marginal increase in pay."

An investor's job is to take money and turn it into more money by backing value creators.

Startup leaders need to accept that investors and stakeholders are going to pressure them, occasionally, into doing things that aren't right for their company. There are times when you are going to have to give in to them. But ultimately, you answer for your company's success at the end of the day. If you feel that a bit of advice isn't right for your business, then you need to be comfortable enough with being uncomfortable to say no to the big and powerful.

PiedPiper manufactures in America, which is rare in general, but our investors kept saying, "When you get to a certain size, you're going to need to build your product in China."

"But, no, we don't," we said bravely, heroes among men.

"But yes," they said, "because we backed another company just like yours and XYZ thing happened, so we had to start building in China."

When this kind of thing takes place, you're at a standoff with your investors. What happens?

Consider the benefits of this investor: contacts via networking and, you know, *money*. If all they can give you is money, then they are not incentivizing you to *not* spend money in the way that you want. If you'll recall, capital can kill. This is one of the ways.

Investors may also encourage you to move to San Fran,[9, 10] and they want you to hire these great, expensive people. But is that what's best for your business?

Their requests can be intimidating if your investors are the reason Slack or Salesforce exist. But if you're considering the health of the organization first, then you have to look past the fog of their clout and give them a good healthy dose of "hell no" every once in a while.

When Is It Time to Hire Someone New?

The pressure to hire new people arises, especially, when companies hit big milestones. The more clients you get, the greater your workload is, and the more work there is to be done. There are three things you need to consider before you can justify bringing on a new team member:

- A proven need in the organization that's been unfulfilled.

- An inability on the part of current team members (due to either mismatched skillset or time management impasses) to fulfill those unaddressed needs.

- The budget to hire a new person.

---

9   The cool kids don't go to Silicon Valley anymore.

10 You're not allowed to call it "San Fran" once you move here, though. It's "SF" or fully "San Francisco." If you call it "San Fran," you're just asking to be treated like a tourist.

The first two are easier to identify, but as we've seen, those are often overlooked. Consider your business's needs—not the needs of your investors or your fellow leaders to look good. These are human beings we're talking about, not decorations or signifiers that you've made it to the big leagues.

Once you've established that your business's needs aren't being met, think about the team members you have access to. In the last chapter, we talked about those tedious tasks that we assume no one else will want. Don't assume. Even if, at this stage in your startup, you're a team of nothing but leaders, you can still reach out to your comrades and see if they might be interested in doing timesheets or whatever else it is that needs to get done.

If no one's available or they just don't have the skills to complete the task that needs to get done—marketing and PR for the company, for example—then it's time to consult your budget to see what you have room for. Now, here's something to consider: just because you have room in the budget to hire someone on full-time right now doesn't mean that you *should*. Finances are finicky. You have the budget this year, but you have no idea what the next year will bring. Will it help your company to hire on a new full-time team member, or will it be the reason you run out of funds next year?

Hop on Fiverr or UpWork to review the available freelancers. It's a higher hourly cost, but it'll save you quite a lot in the long run. As a small company, your digital marketing needs, just as an example, are also fairly minuscule. Someone can get the work done in ten or fifteen hours for the month. That'll save you loads.

If you come to a point where freelancing won't get the job done, then it's time to think about scrounging up the funds to pay for a yearly salary, but really, this should be a last resort. A small team of passionate experts is better than a large team of disillusioned average workers.

Before you bring in a new team member, you have to consider the impact that action will have on the existing team.

What does bringing new people onto the team look like? How do we assimilate them and socialize them with the rest of the organization (which, actually, comes to a stop too when someone new comes in)? If you have non-leader team members at this stage of your business, then let them weigh in on your hiring decision. It'll make them feel valued, and they'll appreciate the effort you're making. It's an activity that not only improves team-member-to-team-member relationships and the quality of the work but also the amount of loyalty your team has for you and your leadership.

Raising the Money to Hire Someone New

Investors love to pressure you to hire new people, but they're not so fond of offering *more* funds to help on that front. You have to raise money at this point to justify hiring someone new. It's a whole salary after all. It's money that you're committed to spending *yearly*, and it's not cheap.

I think of fundraising like it's a marketing campaign. You need to fill the top of the funnel. You need to work out what that flow is going to look like. How do you convert them? The bottom of the funnel is them putting money into your company.

I build the list of prospective investors and look at how they invested in companies like mine. In PiedPiper's case, we're a storage company. I look at my list and ask, "Have they invested in storage before? Have they made money out of a storage company? Are they still invested in a storage company?" If they're still invested in a storage company, I probably don't want to go and talk to them. I don't want to disclose information that could be potentially confidential.

If they've made a lot of money from a storage company that went public and they don't hold any shares with them anymore, then they're a prime candidate to ask for money. They can also be harsh because they may try to compare you to their previous experience, like, "Oh yeah, I see that you said this, but the thing that we saw worked really well at Blah Storage is when we did it this complete other way. We think you guys should do it this way instead." Beware of these investors. Sometimes new startup leaders hear "Yes, if" from investors who are really saying "No, unless." Assuming that you can get their money, that conversation then translates itself into the boardroom and sounds like, "No, no, no, no, no, you guys are doing this all wrong."

I have some investors, though, who are amazing on my board. I'm a huge fan of my biggest investor, and he's a huge fan of me. When he sends me a Christmas greeting, it's all very friendly, but that's also because we're killing it at PiedPiper. If we were bombing and basically flushing his money down the toilet, it might be a very, very different set of circumstances. All that to say, your current investors can also be a great place to mine for the cash to hire a new person. If you have a good relationship with your investors and you can make a good argument for needing more money, then they're likely to give in to your request.

How to Know Someone Is a Good Hire

I'm not a big believer in seven-stage interviews with programming tests and all of that stuff. That doesn't help you in the early stages of a company. It's another reason why you shouldn't do something because that's the process at Google or wherever. Maybe you're trying to find out really specific features like skillset. Would I hire a creative person without having them show me some of their work? No way. I'd never hire an art director without seeing some examples of their art direction. I'd never hire a copywriter without having them write some copy for me. But I've been properly fooled by people who are amazing interviewers. I've left an interview like, "Oh my God, this person is gonna change my life!" and then I got them in the organization just to discover it was all a show. Interviewing is a skill that people can learn. They're not as telling as you think they are.

So how can you avoid that? How can you tell if someone is nothing but a good interviewer and keep from hiring the wrong person?

You have to spend more time with the person as a person. After countless failures (some of which I'll get into in upcoming chapters), I've learned that, before I hire someone at a VP level, I need to spend about ten hours with them at a minimum. That's not necessarily ten hours doing interviews, but I would probably have a meal with them, talking about the job, about the things that they've done, without it being a never-ending list of questions.

If you're in interview mode, you know that someone's going to say something to you along the lines of, "Tell me about a time in a previous role when you were met with a challenge with a teammate and what you did to overcome it." You'll open your mouth and spit out your pre-canned response. We all have one of those, don't we? We're like, "I did this thing, and I'll tell you the three things that were really good about it."

That sends a message to the interviewer and makes them say, "Wow, you can clearly learn from your mistakes. Come on board!"

It's a bit like dating. You probably don't think you're in love after the first date. You haven't got quite enough information. You need some more dates before you realize that person is going to make this huge impact in your life. I think it's really unfair to put someone in an interview for an hour and go, "Yes" or "No." Instead, it's important to discover what that person is like as a human being.

You've got to get to a point in the conversation where you understand what the prospective hire cares about *outside* of work. From there, you can get into a totally different track of conversation.

You might get it by saying, "So, tell me, what do you do outside of work?" but they'll probably say, "Well, I'm married, and I have two kids, and we basically do whatever the kids want," or they'll say some overly generic safe answer.

They're not going to say, "I'm single, and I go crazy every weekend by consuming my body weight in Molly." No one's going to say that even if that is what they do.

But my point is, you can tell a lot about people's values by learning about what they do in their spare time. Take those super cheesy dating profiles as an example: "I like meeting new people" means you're willing to play the numbers game. "I like going out" means you do so excessively. If they list "hiking" as their most active hobby, then they have walked a neighborhood trail exactly one time in the last six months, but they got some cool pictures for the 'Gram from it.

Similar code phrases can be heard in job interviews. The true "work hard, play hard" people don't mention "playing hard" at all. "I like live music" means your hobbies include going to music festivals and not sleeping for three days straight. "Homebody" is a red flag because people are usually lying when they say this; this phrase can mean that they are partiers *or* that they are workaholics, but they don't want to just come out and say that. "Workaholic" can absolutely be a red flag[11] because it can mean that they don't know what they're doing during the workday so they're busting their ass at night to catch up. Working hard is a great quality, but the *why* behind that hard work *is also important.*

The best thing to do is find a person who is a good culture fit already, someone who is primed and ready to be submerged in your organizational environment because it's not

---

[11] However, it's difficult for me to say so outright because I am a workaholic myself—but just because that's what I am doesn't necessarily mean that's what I'm looking for in a new hire.

so different from the one that they're familiar with. You've got to look at someone's personality when they come into the organization and identify early on where the issues are likely to arise.

I'm thinking about two things when I'm hiring people: can they do their job, number one, and number two, can they do it at a level that we need them to?

I just hired a young guy as VP of product, but he'd never been a VP in his life. We saw the dangers of that in my opening example. Even though there's a first time for everything, if the person isn't up for the task, if they don't understand what's required of them in their new role, you may not want your job to be their first experience. The new VP is in the weeds right now when he needs to be at 70,000 feet. Training him is a process, but that's okay because we knew that going in. The thing that I worked out quickly with him was that he works his tail off. He was willing to take interviews at 10:00 p.m. at night, his time. To me, there was no question that the guy *liked* to work and was passionate about our mission.

When I made the decision to bring him on, I thought about that from his perspective (what his drive and desires were), and then I considered how he would fit onto the team and who in the organization he might bond with. Who has the potential to be his work BFF? That's really important as we started to grow the team. It was almost like building a house of cards. You can't just stack them all on top of each other. You want each card to reinforce another card.

You might be worried about knocking your house of cards down because the person is super opinionated and might knock some things out of place. This could be a reason for you *to* bring on this prospective hire. They might come in fully charged while your team members are at 60 percent and inspire people to get their shit together. Either way, it's something you have to consider to set your new employee up for success.

If people are just coming in to clock in and collect benefits, then these people should just fuck off over to Facebook, because they probably have way better benefits than we do and won't expect as much work. We're looking for people who love the work first, who can see the vision as we see it. At the end of the day, to really weed out the people who aren't right for you, you have to be willing to put in work in the interview process as well. Follow your gut; that's part of being comfortable with being uncomfortable: being present enough to hear your intuition and then follow it.

Nurturing Team Members, Old and New

New people want to effect change. They want to make an impact. That's a very natural thing for them to want to do, especially if you bring somebody in at a senior or a managerial level and above. The first thing they're going to do is look for something that they can own and rip up. They're thinking, "I'm going to come in and clean this place up." From their perspective, they've walked in and there's a pile of dirt in the corner, but actually, in some instances, it wasn't a pile of dirt; it was a pile of fertilizer that's valuable to the company. The new person starts cleaning it up, and the rest of the team members are thinking, "Hey, we were saving that! That was our fertilizer to help us grow!"

Now, if you can help your new hire understand what everyone does in the organization, then they can form personal connections. When they want to make their changes or question the process or do all of these reasonably natural behaviors, they're viewed as a person and not a judgmental threat. First, the new person needs to understand what the culture is, which is much harder to teach if the current team members don't really understand it.

I had very, very young adult employees, nineteen-year-olds, and it's a real challenge in and of itself to make sure that it doesn't end up becoming an episode of *Love Island*. Those things need to be managed, but if you identify them early enough, you can actually start to bring people into the teams in a very natural fashion and grow the culture. That way, you don't end up with cliques.

Some startups are wary of hiring these young team members because younger millennials and Gen Zers have the tendency to job hop. Letting go of someone and hiring someone new can be expensive, so they think, "Shoot, I don't have the budget to hire the Edward Snowden of computer geeks. Woe is me; I'll have to settle for these youths."

I don't have much of an issue with people who might be coming into my organization with the idea of using it as a stepping stone to future success, which yes, tends to happen when you have younger, freshly graduated team members. If someone comes in wanting to beat it in a short period of time, I could turn that around and say, "You know what? Okay.

I'm going to get my pound of flesh out of you in the eighteen months to two years that you're going to be here." Now, I do try to make that a mutually beneficial thing by being straight up and asking outright, "How can I make you really valuable to the next place you get to?"

My experience has been that those people don't leave at that point. What actually happens is they gain all this attention, education, and experience, and they think, "Wait, why would I leave? I want to stay here. I love this place."

As long as you're honest and genuine in your approach, you can foster loyal, lifelong team members.

Coming Home from the Honeymoon

Okay, so, your new hire has joined the team and assimilated to the culture, and everyone's super happy. It's like the honeymoon period in a relationship: you think nothing bad can happen. "We're going to be married forever!"

That's when the conflict starts to arise.

They didn't hit the sales targets that they said that they would hit. The product launch is late. They're not able to translate the software updates into hardware updates. The list goes on. Whatever it is, you thought hiring this person was going to solve all of these problems. Then, it becomes volatile because you gave this money, in the way of a salary, on the premise that they would do what you said to do.

While it was 100 percent on them to do their due diligence to voice when they believed they couldn't meet these milestones, it was also on you to check in with them to make sure they had everything they needed to do the job properly.

You might have been like, "Yes, So-and-so, I'd like you to do this task in this order like one, two, three," but then when they did that task, it looked like two, one, three, and it rubbed you the wrong way. But does it really make that much of a difference? Probably not. Maybe there's a reason for them doing it that way, and you should let them get on with it.

If it's a real issue then, okay, challenge that, but understand your motivations. New managers and leaders need to learn to not just poke the bear because they think it needs to be poked. Step away.

You'll be surprised by what people will achieve on their own, especially if you've done a good job of hiring smart people. There's that classic Steve Jobs quote: "It doesn't make sense to hire smart people and tell them what to do; we hire smart people so they can tell us what to do." This is a time when listening to the people in big tech might pay off. (But remember to investigate the needs of your business before copying the greats.)

Scaling Your Team to Your Business

At PiedPiper, we have learned our lessons about hiring the wrong people (or hiring the right people to do the wrong job). We've learned that we need to find like-minded people to work at our company. To be successful, we need people with a similar mindset to work with us to build our culture.

Know when it's time to expand. Think about the next scaling step, not just the one that you're in. What decisions might you make today that will get reinforced at the next step? Is hiring someone outside of your organization the best idea for scaling, or might it be better to keep multitasking? Or should you hire a freelancer? Make sure that while you're thinking ahead, you don't get ahead of yourself. If you're not a public company, don't act like a public company. Just because you have the money to hire new people right now doesn't mean you need new people. Don't go bankrupt trying to look like a big company when you're not (yet).

Understand the difference between what is valuable to your customers and what is valuable to leadership. It's okay for people to continue wearing multiple hats for now. You need to be a good leader to learn how to properly scale and motivate your team.

CHAPTER 6

LEADERSHIP

PIEDPIPER HAS HAD A HORRIFIC TRACK RECORD OF LOSING VPS OF product. I think we're on number five or six at this point. It's not unique to have high turnover in a specific role in an organization. A friend of mine works for a company that has a telehealth platform, and they've gone through exactly the same process with their head of design; they're on number seven.

At PiedPiper, we've definitely brought in some duds, people we never should have hired, but we've also hired people who were completely competent, who have done this before in the same industry at larger companies. Seeing some great people go has caused me to sit down with the rest of the leadership team and ask two questions:

- "Are we actually ready for this role? Or are we trying to fill a box in the org chart?", and then

- "Is there any behavior that we need to change in our leadership for this person to be successful? Has the reason that all the other people failed have nothing to do with them and everything to do with us?"

We were previously hiring to fill a box in the org chart, which, as we've seen in the last chapter, I oppose. Don't hire someone until there's actually a need to hire them, meaning the role can't be fulfilled by the current team. The first few hires and fires could have been chalked up to that issue—we were hiring outside of the organization for the wrong reasons.

With the latter half of the hires, though, the problem seemed to be that the VPs of product weren't being empowered to fulfill their role by the person who had been previously filling the spot.

This is fairly common in a SaaS company: someone built something (anything as simple as a widget or as complex as a full app) and, in their mind, owned the product from that moment on. It's usually a founder, and the product was their idea in the first place. That's their baby, if you think about it, so it's hard to then hand that over to someone else. You don't just go and give your baby away.

When a new person comes in and reaches their hands out for the product, the founder (or whoever) silently screams, "No, that's mine! I want to care for and feed it. I can't trust that you're going to care for it the way I would." It can get emotional, for sure.

One of the founders of the telehealth company is not a designer in the true sense, or they have no formal design training, but they care deeply about the aesthetic of the product. So, they've ended up shadowing the head of design. They've always wanted to dictate how things were done, and they continued to do so even after the new person came on board. As a result, people continued to look to the founder to make the decisions or to provide input, completely usurping the head of design's authority.

At PiedPiper, the product that the product owners kept trying to own had been owned by the CTO at the time. Ed was technically part of the interview process, but he wasn't fully present in the process because he believed we were simply hiring a VP to fill a box in the org chart. He felt like his role was being diminished more than he was being helped (by having his schedule freed up). If he had been more engaged in the interviews and learned to trust each new hire, he could have actually slept at night, instead of staying up late doing this other job too. Instead of recognizing the issue between—I don't know—the first five VPs of product, Ed would reassume the role as interim VP of product after each official VP of product left PiedPiper.

See how messy that is? Almost unequivocally, the VPs of product failed because they never got in sync and in tune with the perspective and opinions of the shadow VP of product, aka the CTO. The incoming VPs looked outside at the industry before they looked inside at what we, as a company, were trying to do. Inevitably, we'd reach a point of conflict, with both sides implying, "No, you're an idiot. You don't know what you're talking about. We're trying to do something completely different," but with an inability to actually verbalize or document what we were trying to do. It was a complete impedance: our VPs of product never lined up with the views of the CTO, who was also a founder of the company.

We had a problem: a high-paid person wasn't performing and was, in some instances, causing more damage in the organization. That ultimately led us to exit those people, even in the instance where one of those candidates was a personal friend of a few of us, including the CTO.

Some of the blame must go to the CTO (who is now the CEO and has made peace with his past mistakes). The VP of product was not enabled to actually manage the product because every decision that they made was either second-guessed by the CTO or by the rest of the team. When you're not empowered to do your job, you just get to a point where you say, "Fuck it. It doesn't matter what I say. My opinion doesn't matter. Everyone's just going to listen to the boss."

I eventually had to tell him, "Hey, look, you're part of the problem." I was the right person to do this with him because we were so close—we had been roommates and started (and failed) other companies together. There was trust between the two of us, even when there wasn't trust between Ed and each VP of product. It wasn't just the CTO's fault; it was also mine because I enabled him to keep hold of the product for so long.

He should have been more closely guided to let go of the product by the CEO. The VP of product never took ownership of the product, which meant they were destined to fail from the start. This is a huge leadership issue.

Team Leadership and Trust

There are two layers of leadership: leadership of the organization and team leadership. Team leadership is different from management, which is essentially asking your team members, "Are you doing a good job? Do you show up on time? Do you follow the policies?" Team leadership is helping your team members grow, as much as it's about showing them how to do things and walking through the process. It's letting them take things on, knowing they might screw it up. It's a tender thing. It's about trust, ultimately.

Say I asked a team member to take care of this thing, whatever it is. If they fucked it up, I have to fix it. I have to get comfortable with the amount of engagement that it's going to take to watch them closely enough to provide support if they need help but keep enough distance to empower them to make their own decisions. I need to be confident enough in my own abilities to recover the ball if they drop it.

As the leader of a team, you're a quiet observer. When you see something going sideways, count to ten. Give your team member the opportunity to catch it on their own and get it right—but don't wait so long that you set them up for failure. Failure is an excellent teacher (we'll go over that later), but only if it's organic. You can't orchestrate a failure and expect your team member to be grateful for the manufactured lesson. If there aren't any real stakes, no one's going to learn anything. At that point, it's just about stroking your own ego, which is self-serving and, inherently, not great leadership.

Trust in a relationship has to be bidirectional; it can't just be them trusting you or you trusting them. If you trust them but they don't trust you—unfortunately a common manager/subordinate relationship dynamic—both sides lose. Many people don't trust their managers because they believe their managers only do things for their own benefit. If they trust you, but you don't trust them, you become a micromanaging nightmare. You absolutely need mutual trust: your organization is a collective of connected people. If those people are instead disjointed parts, then nothing amazing will come forth. If these parts are working together, then you can change the world.

Mistakes New Leaders Make

I see this with junior leaders all the time: they'll say, "I'm going to do a weekly one-on-one with every person in my team." That's admirable, given the emphasis we placed on trust in the last section. But let's take a second to do the math here. Say you have seven people. If you spend an hour with each person, you now work four days a week. Why give up a full day like that?

"Well, I want to make sure they're happy," the juniors will say, "and I want to make sure that nothing gets away from me."

But when they have these weekly mandatory meetings, the opposite happens: they're inadvertently training their direct reports that they're going to get an audience each week, teaching them to rely on authority to make decisions and disempowering them.

Weekly meetings are a strategic move for people who are more concerned with securing their role in the company, but it's not a good move for the company. What's good for the company must, and can, be good for each and every team member.

Instead, set expectations for your team members and trust them to get it done. You *must* trust them to get it done because you can't be everywhere at once. You have to stick with your area, to ensure that area of the company stays healthy, and trust that others are doing the same. But do come up for air occasionally to make sure all the areas are being cared for in the right ways.

These junior leaders also fall into another trap: they don't put up boundaries. You have to say, "You guys can't just pick up the phone and call me whenever you want. Please just Google it."

An interesting dynamic happens when you grow really fast and bring people up to speed quickly. It feels like the easiest way to do that is to spend lots of time with them, but actually, sometimes the best thing to do is not spend any time with them and let them work it out. Otherwise, you just end up with a bunch of people who want to call you every five minutes.

Empower people to make decisions without you. If your inferiors have to wait to run things by you before they do things, no one will get anything done. They can't be waiting for you. It feels like you're delinquent because it *looks* like you're not actively doing something and you feel like you should be. But if you spoon-feed everyone, then they are going to come to expect that. These employees are not your babies; they're full-grown adults who can do it themselves, damnit.

New leaders also have a hard time being vulnerable in front of their team members. Being a leader means being able to fail, in public, without an ego. When you fail and own up to your mistakes, you show your team members that it's okay to be human. No one's perfect. And, in fact, being that willing to show your faults to your team members can help them trust you. From there, you can form the relationship you need to in order to succeed.

Mistakes Experienced Leaders Make

New leaders aren't the only people making mistakes in start-ups, though.

I mentioned in the first chapter that all you really have to do as a startup leader is go from zero to one. This concept comes from Peter Thiel and basically means you have to go from *not* being a company to *being and staying* a company. Your business is a company, or it's not; it's a yes-or-no question, a binary issue. Leader*ship*, however, is on a spectrum.

If, as a company, you feel like you've made it from zero to one, then more needs to be done to maintain your company, meaning there are more responsibilities, which usually get delegated to other team members. As a zero-to-one leader, you have to let new people do their job and fulfill those responsibilities; otherwise, you're just juggling all these hats, letting the brims block out the larger visions, and you're just at 1.1, so to speak, which isn't a thing in business. There's not enough literature you can write (or read) to address the way (even experienced) leaders don't know how to delegate—but that's not the only mistake they make.

Others include:

- Not understanding what needs to be done *in order to* delegate it.

- Being unable to see the big picture.

- Thinking, "What got us here will get us there."

- Micromanaging, which is a roundabout way of saying "harboring distrust."

Just as humans aren't inherently good or bad, leaders aren't all good or bad. Ed wasn't acting like a good leader to the VPs of product, but ultimately, he *is* a great leader because I was able to approach him and give him my insights. That's not always the case, as you'll see in a moment. A good leader should be able to sit with the discomfort of negative feedback and lean into that conflict with professionalism.

Get Comfortable with Conflict

As a leader, you need to have three-sixty awareness, which just isn't possible to do unless you've found a way to get comfortable in the discomfort of your role in your company. You need to understand the business's needs, your personal needs, your collective team's needs, and each of your direct report's needs.

When you're leading a team of people—even if it's just *two* people—it's impossible to please everybody. There are times when you have to stand your ground, whether it's a personal thing or you just genuinely believe it's the best thing for the company.

You can't lead teams and manage people if you're not willing to put yourself in the line of some conflict.

That doesn't mean yelling and screaming. Obviously not. You can't be aggressive to people you work with. Generally, it ends badly—lawsuits and terminations.

Getting comfortable with conflict means that if you work with someone who you've become friendly with, you might have to call them out occasionally and say, "You done gone and fucked that up, bud."

That can be a very difficult thing to do. It's a super delicate balance because conflict can manifest as passive-aggressiveness if you're *too* worried about coming off aggressively.

Without friction, though, you can't polish a surface. You need that little bit of friction, the checking of assumptions, the checking of each other, and the checking of ourselves to do something good. No one just wakes up and goes, "I've got this amazing idea!" and then it becomes the next big thing.

It just looks like that because you only hear about companies, like Facebook and Apple, once they've already made it, but it's never like that. There's not a single example on the planet that looks like that. The closest you would get is striking oil in Texas, where you could dig a hole in your backyard, like, "Hey, look at that! There's a black swimming pool now, and we're rich!" Or maybe winning the lottery is like that, though I don't know anyone, even adjacently, who has won the lottery.

Anytime anyone builds something, it's a bloody, hard process to get there, to *make it*. All of those little conflicts and indecisions and hard decisions make your company's success possible, and comfortability with conflict is just a part of that process.

How I Became the COO at PiedPiper

Being a CEO in a startup is surprisingly lonely. People claim to be on your side—the investors, the executive staff, the VPs and managers—but often they'd just as quickly replace or betray you, to fulfill their own agenda, as support you. Truth is, for the most part you're on your own. At times, there are dynamics of the organization that you can't share, a weight that you carry on your shoulders alone. Consider reaching a point where you have to tell everyone, "Shit, guys, we're running out of money, so we can't afford to pay everyone next month." You make the call because everyone's relying on you, but you can't always rely on everyone. The responsibility means you have to work freaking hard. And, you have to surround yourself with people you trust.

If you're the founder/CEO, the vision is yours. If you've been brought in so the founders can be innovative and visionary while you run the company, you have to buy into their vision, even if it's not your *exact* vision, because if you can't buy into it, you won't be able to do your job for long.

The old CEO of PiedPiper, Charles, was compensated in such a way that he didn't need to buy into the vision of the company. Don't get me wrong; Charles is a nice man, and this isn't a personal affront. He got paid whether his heart was in it or not, and it wasn't. The crux of the story is that his first job with PiedPiper was managerial in nature. He was co-president, but functionally, he was the general manager.

Our founding CEO made a career out of starting companies and then stepping out of the way; his passion is company creation, not continuity. Charles had a similar mindset, so it's not surprising he was chosen to replace the founding CEO.

When Charles came into the role, he said, "I'm going to go and make all of this money, and it'll be great! I'm going to hire all these people!" but he never bought into the company strategy.

Charles was looking for the short-term value outcome: "What is the one thing we can do today or in the very near future that will help us sell the company?" It's not the thing you need to do to take the company public, to help the company thrive on its own. He was looking for more immediate gratification and couldn't see the bigger picture. He wasn't operating with the company—or the team members who did share the company vision—in mind. All the tasks that a CEO actually needs to complete? Charles kicked that can down the road. Take funding, for example.

Charles's message was, "I'm not going to make a decision on that today because we need funding," but then he didn't do his part to obtain the funding. So, in his mind, he thought, *Great, I don't have to make that decision today. I'm giving the people a light at the end of the tunnel: I'm letting them know that I'm thinking about funding. I'm doing my job by thinking about funding!* That tactic went on for years with incremental finance being done through other mechanisms.

Flash forward: I'd been in Europe for a couple of weeks doing a roadshow for work, and I was in my hotel room in Stockholm when Ed, the CTO, called me. He said, "Hey, the chairman of the board basically asked me to be CEO. He said Charles's not working out and asked if I wanted to do it. I think it's the right thing for the business, but if we do so, I'm going to need you to basically pick up all of the operational aspects of PiedPiper. People are getting tired; bills are getting high. There's money in the bank account but not a lot."

Ed let me in on what that conversation would look like with Charles, the timing, what his thoughts were from a recovery perspective, and what the general sentiment was of the boardroom.

And I said, "That's what I want to do anyway." I had been looking at Charles and thinking to myself, *This guy's a bit of a show*. I had already known that we were running out of money because I was being told, "Hey, don't go buying too much equipment unless you ask me, okay?" I knew I could probably do a better job of leading the company, within bounds. Given the opportunity, I'm generally not someone who's shy of taking on the challenge.

I told Ed I'd do whatever he wanted because he and I had worked together seventeen or eighteen years by this point and knew each other very well. We'd lived together; we'd gone through personal challenges together. We'd faced a lot of adversity. I trusted him, and career-wise, it was the right thing to do. I knew how hard I was willing to work, and the ideas that I had brought to Charles hadn't been heard.

In parallel, Charles, the CEO, was still very much around. This always happens: there's the behind-the-scenes, and there's the front of the house.

The next day, I flew from Stockholm to London, and I was in the Heathrow lounge when Charles called me. He was driving to work, and he said, "I've got a couple ideas I want to run by you," and then we just started chatting about how we could raise some money for the company.

I said, "Here's an idea. It may be useful. I'll get back onsite, and we'll just lock ourselves in a room, and we'll work it out. None of us are really quitters, so we're just going to work it out. How hard can it possibly be? People raise money for stupid shit all the time. We've got a real thing. We built a real business. It's really difficult to do, and we've done it. How do we *not* get money?"

In the back of my head, I knew that his head was pretty close to the chopping block at this point, from a boardroom perspective. I obviously had to use my discretion. I couldn't show any sign of weakness or insubordination or anything like that. Also, I genuinely wanted to help the guy because, even if he did get fired, I knew the work wasn't for waste because the first thing we would do is raise money.

He agreed it was a good idea.

I said, "Cool, I'll be back next week. I'll organize something," and then I asked him—and this is the bit that really sticks with me—"What is it that I can do so you can focus 100 percent of your energy on raising the rounds?"

I was greeted with stony silence, followed by a blatant, final, "I don't know." And that told me everything I needed to know about the future—what would happen to Charles, what would happen to Ed and to me. I thought, *Oh, okay, this guy is so disassociated from all the problems that he can't see the wood for the trees.*

Everything he did for the organization created absolutely zero value, smoke and mirrors to divert everyone's attention from the work he wasn't doing. Because of all of the issues he caused, we were doomed. I was glad to know that there was a backup plan in process.

I had that call with Charles on Friday, and I landed back in California that weekend. Charles, Ed, and I got together the next week in an off-site meeting room. We sat down and said, "Okay, look, this isn't that hard. Let's get a shared Google Doc going. We know the narrative. We know what an investment pitch needs to look like."

It's well-trodden territory at this point: ten to fifteen slides in a deck. What's the market? What's the problem? What's the solution? What's the traction? How much money do we want? An eighteen-year-old kid can put a pitch together. It's not beyond the way of man. We had three smart guys. Charles used to be an investor. We'd all raised money before. We just needed to get our story together.

"We'll talk about this. What about that? Let's test that assumption, pressure test that." I looked across the table at Ed, and Ed looked across the table at me, and we were in the Google Doc, writing down good ideas, and there was stuff going up on the whiteboard. I was thinking, *We might just save this whole thing*.

We went out for lunch. We didn't chat about work too much. We got back and just hit a wall in the afternoon. We all went off to different corners of the room to do some solo brainstorming; we were all equally fried. At one point, I stopped and looked up: Charles was staring at a blank whiteboard. It was like, *Whew, boy, that's not a good sign*. He was supposed to be the visionary. *He was the CEO*, the one who was supposed to be like, "Follow *me*, lads." Even if it wasn't even a fully formed idea, he was the one who should have been leading us to victory. There was literally nothing going on.

After getting not much else done, we decided, "This is going to be a two-day process. We'll all come back tomorrow."

As we were leaving, Charles muttered, "Yeah, maybe I'll just call you guys in the morning, and we'll decide if we want to come in." Another bad omen.

In the morning, quite early, came an email from Charles: *Hey, I'm going to work from home today. Let's sync up later about where we think we're at with the deck. I've got the business to be worrying about, plenty of things to do Thursday and Friday. Let's connect sometime after the weekend.* I put a meeting on our group calendar for 11:00 a.m. Monday.

The deep-voiced narrator made another appearance to say: *there was nothing going on. Charles had lost it.*

Ed and I knew Charles was probably going to get fired on Monday.

In the meantime, Ed and I kept working on the deck. We'd both had some time to think about it, and we'd done some more work on it. We asked ourselves, "What do you think—should we keep going? What happens if he gets fired before our meeting with him on Monday?"

He walked into the office on Monday, so we all sat down to the eleven o'clock meeting, and I figured it wasn't happening today and was curious to see what he had to say. Charles began, "So I thought about this over the weekend. And I think the thing that we need to do is restructure the business. We can cut costs if we get rid of all of these people, so let's just double down on this part of engineering."

And he looked dead at me and said, "How much would we save if we just didn't do any marketing for a little while?"

And I said, "Well, sure, we'd save some money that way. But those people are all contractors. They're all personal friends of mine. It'll really hurt them if we suddenly cancel all their contracts. In a lot of instances, we represent upwards of a third of their work. They're not going to be able to fill that tomorrow."

I understood that people sometimes need to be let go. We covered that in another chapter. Charles, Ed, and I were very clear about what was and what wasn't fair game at this meeting. The biggest problem I saw, if we just up and let these contractors go, would be losing every single one of them in the long term. We would prove to them that we were an unreliable source of income, and we'd never get them back. And I had already tapped into my friend network so we could get cheap marketing.[12] Why should we lose all of that?

"Well, what about the engineers?" Charles said. "Could we let any of them go?"

If we had let any of the engineers go, we would have been completely fucked. As soon as we let one engineer go, they'd all get skittish. Engineers are very fragile creatures. We would have spooked the herd by letting even one or two go, and they would all start looking for other jobs—and if you're in the tech business, you know engineers don't stay unemployed for long.

---

12 I was getting them out of Australia and paying them in US dollars. They thought that they were getting a great hourly rate, and we were getting a 25 percent discount.

We'd be sore out of luck when we wanted to hire again. And I was thinking, *I'm going to probably start looking for another job based on what's going on here because shit just doesn't make any sense.*[13]

Then Charles said, "I think I've got thirty days before I get shot in the head. I'm trying to work out what I can turn around in the next thirty days." Ultimately, it would have been his decision if that's what he'd wanted to do, although it would never have happened because of the previous conversations Ed had had with the board. When Charles said, "I've got days left," Ed actually turned around and said, "I want to be really straight with you. I think you've got less than a week." Charles was a bit stunned.

After our meeting (where nothing was decided), Charles was asked to call the chairman, and the chairman advised him that his services were no longer required. We had to make an announcement to the team. We had to explain to the team, "Our CEO's just been fired." We needed to reassure them that we were doing something to sustain the business.

Because that's what leaders do.

Owning the Product, Taking Responsibility

After the CTO of PiedPiper became the CEO and I became the COO, we started to interview the person we eventually

---

13 Obviously, I didn't leave—see the title of this section. I think it's important to include this thought in the story, though, because that's how people in your organization are going to start thinking if they smell blood in the water. I could double my salary if I sold my soul and went to work for Lizard Boy, and that's what you're up against as a startup leader: the benefits the devil can offer. Be better than the devil by holding space for trust and compassion.

hired as our current VP of product. There was a conversation between myself and the CEO that went along the lines of, "I think we should acknowledge that we have been as responsible for the failure of the previous VPs of product as they have been in this role. If we want this person to work out, we have to change our behavior because we can't just expect them to come in and not suffer the fate of their predecessors. We don't have anybody else to blame."

As startup leaders, you have to ask yourselves, "Are we actually going to own the role all the way through that job?" It's likely that you don't have the capacity to take on that role; otherwise, you would save yourself some coin. If you don't want to own the role and its responsibilities, you have to relinquish the whole thing. At PiedPiper, we now have a conversation on a regular basis that goes, "I think you need to let So-and-so come up with their suggested answers, and then let's review what that looks like before we enact a decision."

It doesn't help the company if the leadership member who once filled that role now force-feeds decisions to the new team member who has taken on those responsibilities.

Now that the VP of product works for me, I have a duty to make that person as successful as I possibly can. And that also means that I, at times, might not say much right until the point that I see that something potentially bad is going to happen. It might mean being able to communicate the new plan the VP came up with to a wider group. I need to show them that I have their back and that I trust them to do their job.

Lead the Way the Right Way

There are times when I accept that we aren't doing some things very well at PiedPiper, yet it's not my area of expertise. They're not my team members, so involving me to reorganize doesn't improve the situation since I'm not going to deal with those individuals in the long haul. I don't have the foggiest idea about the full history of working with those people, nor do I have any instinct regarding the way they'll respond to specific changes.

If you don't work on a team, you don't have a three-sixty perspective on what's happening with that team. Therefore, you need to humble yourself and say that you don't necessarily know what's best. You have to trust your junior leaders and your team members. Saying something out of turn to another team leader would be like remarking on another person's relationship. You just see the outside. You don't see that, when they return home, they act totally different with one another, or the manner in which they carry on out in public is just a game they play.

It's similar at the big-tech organizations as well. Leaders show the side they need you to see; they're not giving up their insider leadership tips and tricks.

When we stop to remember that culture is this truly precious thing that happens naturally, we'll understand we're trying to force productivity at the expense of the most valuable thing that we have in the association: the team. The people. Lead your organization with trustworthiness and genuineness and help your team members grow. It's to your greatest advantage.

CHAPTER 7

FIND YOUR REPLACEMENT

I MET ROBIN THE FIRST TIME I WENT TO THE BOMBAWORKS OFFICES IN Berlin. Of the folks on the BombaWorks team, I spent the most time with Robin, dealing with the paralysis-perfectionism narrative. Each time I went to Berlin, he was the guy who would say, "Hey, let's all go out for dinner after this." Over time our friendship formed.

Later, the BombaWorks guys needed some space in California to perform assembly work to support one of the trials they were doing for a big-tech campus. I was at PiedPiper by then, and we had a facility with a factory. I volunteered to put them up. I had even more time to spend with Robin during his California sojourn. When he started having second thoughts about working for BombaWorks, he sought out my mentorship, and we talked about whether it was the best place for him and his career trajectory.

Some of us are just complete morons, and we do startups

because we love hurting ourselves. But for some, the startup lifestyle is a bit of culture shock: you think it'll be one thing, but then it's another. Robin was in the second category, and not long after that conversation, he left BombaWorks. He'd decided that he wanted to go and do his own thing with a friend of his.

We stayed in contact after that, the cadence of our communication becoming more frequent during the course of a year. The gig with his friend wasn't what he thought it would be either, and he confided in me one day that things weren't as rosy in the startup world as he hoped they would be, but he wasn't sure what next steps he should take.

I said to him, "Look, we're scaling manufacturing at PiedPiper. It'd be great if you could help me set up a bunch of this stuff. I don't have enough time, and I need someone. You're a smart dude, and I trust you. I can hire you as a contractor, and then we'll see where that takes us, but if you're not interested, no hard feelings. If you get offered a job at BMW, Daimler, or Porsche in Germany and you want to go and do that, then cool, man. That's your dream; that's your background. Don't let me get in the way of that."

Robin agreed to join the team, to give my mentorship a chance. Within a year's time, he would take my place at PiedPiper.

Now I don't want to be in my old role anymore because Robin can fill it. I can't best serve my organization in that role anymore. Exceptional leadership means putting the company first, and not surprisingly, it takes exceptional leadership to train your replacement.

What Does Finding Your Replacement Mean?

True mentorship means you're so invested in someone else's career goals that you're investing in them the same way you would do in yourself. Your replacement is not just someone to manage your calendar or to do stuff for you that you can't be bothered to do. It's someone who *you* can genuinely rely on. That's the level of mentorship we're striving for: you want to prep them so well that if you needed to step away from your role for a second, they could pop up into your place to ensure things run smoothly.

A few chapters ago, we spoke about filling the shop with people who are a good culture fit. It's similar to finding your replacement. It's about ensuring the success of the overall business, which is made up of people—people who are smart and capable and share the same values and vision. We also talked about how newer leaders get freaked out when their subordinates seem "too" capable. They get worried that the little guy is coming for their job. Here's a secret for you: there is no little guy. There are people who belong at your company, and there are people who don't. That's it. You're all working for the greater good of the company—or, at least, you should be.

This is a person you're going to load responsibility onto and give a crop of their own to grow. No doubt, you will hand off tedious tasks to them because you need help, but you'll also delegate important work to them, share the responsibility and, therefore, the fulfillment of making things go 'round in your business. You're empowering your replacement to make decisions on their own, so you don't always have to be there.

At this point in your startup leadership career, you probably don't have time to take a real vacation. That's what balancing the pressure was about, finding small moments of reprieve, enjoying "micro-vacations" by taking a stroll around someplace beautiful. If you have someone who understands the INs and OUTs of your role, then you actually can step away. You can enjoy the cushy part of being one of the higher-ups at a business.

Trouble occurs when people reach this level in their organization and struggle to walk away. They've invested so much of themselves into the company and its product, it's challenging to trust someone else to handle it.

You've got to—for the good of the company. You can't be the only person who understands your role because if something should happen to you—good or bad, you might win the lottery and never return—then the company is left stranded. If the company is your passion, then you need a replacement. If your title and salary are your passion, then this book isn't really for you. Those things are nice perks, but for the company to survive, your focus must be on the company and its mission.

I've said it once, and I'll say it again: quit looking at—and trying to copy—those successful big-tech companies. If you stare into the sun too long, you're going to go blind. People get blinded by the success stories. They want the money, the prestige, the name recognition. They're not focused enough on how they can change or impact the world. They're not focused enough on their own business to make their company successful.

And what do we need to do to keep the focus and self-awareness it takes for our company to thrive? Say it with me, crowd—I've stopped singing, and I'm holding the microphone out to you: *you have to get comfortable being uncomfortable.*

By helping your replacement grow, you're helping your company grow—you're making your organization its own entity. It's a living organism, and the workers inside it are its cells. You're just a human being, and if you focus on yourself, the legacy you leave behind will be finite. But your company *can* outlive you. If it's something you're really passionate about, then that's something you should want.

When you find your replacement, you're not putting yourself out of a job. You're making room for your role to evolve, which is to say that you're making room for your organism-ation to grow.

Moving Up the Ranks

I'll use a military analogy again: Every new military recruit goes through basic training, the light beat. The *Full Metal Jacket* types break them down to build them up, mentally. From an office's perspective, new recruits go to boot camp too. The difference is that they're taught to be officers but not better soldiers or pilots. Even still, when the commander in chief changes, the generals change, the admirals change, and all of the levels below that change too. It's an organization continually in flux.

It's not a perfect upward motion, though. You don't end up with someone saying, "I've been a general for thirty years, and I'm ready to do something else," and then the Powers that Be move him somewhere else just like that. He could get a more senior position, but he could also experience a lateral move because someone decided that he wasn't quite ready to go up to the next level. With the corporate world, you get this Hollywood story of people going from the mailroom to the CEO's chair, like, "This is the person who started in the mailroom as an eighteen-year-old kid, and at sixty-five, they were appointed the CEO of this public company."

That is the only way that the military runs its organization. Everybody starts at the equivalent of the mailroom. You join at the bottom. Not everyone can be admirals or generals at the same time, nor should they be, if they don't have the right experience. People's lives are at stake! For the most part, you need some plain old grunts—the people with personality traits that you don't want in the higher-ups. Not everyone is destined to be a leader.

When you look at startups, you'll see we don't generally run like that. We bring people in at different levels. We don't bring everyone in at the bottom, and then, slowly, over twenty-five years, people get promoted to the top. No, we live in a world where people change their jobs a lot more than ever in the world's history. Today, the number of people who would stay with one company for thirty-five years is an imaginary number. It's almost unfathomable for us to even conceptualize it. We wouldn't do that. Our parents' generation worked for one company from eighteen to retirement.

Replacement Eligibility

When employing your replacement, you're going to need someone you can rely on. The last thing you want is for the person you carefully selected as your replacement to fall apart at the seams at the first hurdle they have to jump. They might not do a great job. They might only be able to delay the emergency for a little bit longer, but more than anything, they're going to step in and *try* to deal with it.

Likewise, your replacement needs to know they can rely on you, that you've got their back. Any number of things *will* go wrong. Startups aren't perfect. The *world* isn't perfect—big, scary events happen all the time. When it gets tough, we need to rely on each other.

Reliability is a universal trait that you want in all your employees, whether they'll replace you one day or not. Beyond that, you need to have an idea of the other traits or skills your replacement must have, before you go out looking for one.

You want to get to a point where you don't need to micromanage. You want your replacement to take responsibility for their tasks in an unassuming, unrequested manner. What you're ultimately trying to foster is the same level of trust and competency that you instill across the business.

You should eventually have multiple replacements as you start to gain additional responsibilities. You wear many hats in the early stages, but as the company grows, those hats become individuals or, in some instances, entire departments. In principle, you need to have *at least one* person whom you tacitly trust—and they have to trust you. Someone who would essentially take a bullet for you. If your replacement or mentee saw something going horribly wrong at your business, they wouldn't just let the ball drop. Robin is one of those people.

How to Train Your Replacement

I got to know Robin through a process of continual coaching and trust-building. For example, I stepped in when I saw someone inadvertently (hopefully) trying to take advantage of him. I modeled how to handle those conflicts until I could say, "You just gotta work it out. I don't know what the answer is. No one knows what the answer is. Maybe you should get the hell out." As his mentor, I could coach him, but the decision was his to make.

You can set up guardrails, but you have to leave space for your mentee to swerve and course correct. They're probably going to bump the guardrail, maybe even scrape the fender. There's probably going to be some waterworks at some point, but they're not going to die. The life lesson comes from finding the edge of safety.

I wanted Robin to be able to come in and lead, not because it was a nice thing to do for him, although I did care about him from a personal perspective, but because that was what the organization needed. As my responsibilities increase, I can't keep all the data in my head nor do all the tasks associated with it. The challenge for me is letting go as I hire more people to do more distinct roles. And I'm far more comfortable letting go of something knowing I'm handing it off to someone I trust.

I used to generate all the invoices for the company, but that task got passed down to Robin when I became COO.

Recently, I received an email from one of Robin's team members with the invoices, which meant Robin took the initiative to delegate this task. It's not about delegating the stuff you don't feel like doing. There are parts of the job that are always going to be tedious, but those things still need to be done correctly. Seeing this showed me that he's on his way to being ready for more responsibilities, which is the perfect time to project new visions on the horizon. If you wait until your replacement is "ready" to take on your role, it's too late—because your replacement has already started looking for other job opportunities at that point.

Your replacement learns through trial and error, which is only made possible when you trust them to do their best and can forgive them when they make mistakes. You have to give them an entire length of rope and wait to see what they do with it. Maybe they'll throw it out to team members who are drowning and pull them out of the water. Maybe they'll get tangled up and find that the rope has turned into a noose. Step in. Untie the knot. Then give them space to take the lead again.

When a Replacement Steps In

Right now, PiedPiper is going through a period of hyper-growth. In just nine months, we doubled our organization's size; *loads* of people are joining. All startups, as they hit these peaks in sales, go through a time of hyper-growth, and that could be one to five, or thirty to sixty people. Hyper means different things for different sized companies.

You don't always have the time to go, "Okay, I've got this part of the business, and I want to give it to someone, and I've got someone who's absolutely perfect! We're not going to drop the ball on anything! Because we've been grooming this person for five years to take over that part of the business!" That's what it looks like in a big company, but it can't look like that in a small company. At a startup, people only become C-suite members if a current member steps down or gets the chop—which is how Ed and I joined the C-suite last year at PiedPiper.

When Robin joined the team, I wasn't the COO yet. I was a VP. I worked *really* hard, but I wasn't a C-suite member yet. I wasn't a general at the company at the time, so I didn't have that much responsibility (or that much power). It's not in my nature, but if I wanted to, I could've gotten to the end of the day and said "It's not my problem" when things went wrong. But instead, I had Robin working for me, and he and I would talk every day, and I'd get involved when conflict resolution was needed. I would address conflicts to keep the business moving forward.

In a very short period of time, the CEO was fired, and I became the COO. I inherited a clusterfuck of an organization—it wasn't in compliance, contracts were wrong, paperwork hadn't been filed—you name it. As a result, I didn't have time to incrementally say "Robin, I want you to go and do this one thing now" of something that would have been my responsibility as the VP. I left a void of leadership because I had to. The company needed different things from me. I just told him to take care of as much of my previous responsibilities as he possibly could around production, manufacturing, and the ERP system.

At that point, I only had two jobs to work on. One of them was to put some money in the bank because if we had no money in the bank, we were completely fucked, and number two, I had to get the organization into a state where someone would invest. Those two jobs were really a lot of work, so I told Robin, "I need you to do as much as you possibly can. 'Kay, thanks, bye."

For the most part, he was able to do it, because I had given him quite a lot of exposure to the various parts of the business prior to my stepping into the COO role. After all, he and I had worked very closely over the proceedings by then. I knew he was capable of doing the work—I knew it before I hired him, but I trusted him to do the job, capably, professionally, because of the time I had spent training him.

There are now company processes that exist because Robin implemented them. After taking on more and more responsibility and continuing to prove himself, he got to a place of more seniority because people are going, "Oh, actually, Jason, Ed, or whoever else is not the authority on that matter. Robin is the authority." That's a true replacement, and it happened because of the time Robin spent training with me and my willingness to let go and let him step in.

Find Your Replacement—for the Sake of Your Company

If you're thinking about this from an "I need to be needed to be successful" point of view, then the business itself is going to fail. If you consider the business's needs first, then your needs take a backseat, but the company will thrive as a result.

Finding your replacement is leaning into your asymmetric advantage. This person has the power to uproot you. They could potentially show you up, make you seem like you're not the right person to lead your company. But you have a position in this company for a reason; only you know what you know, and no one has your vantage point. In training your replacement, you're giving yourself room to look at the big picture and relieve yourself of daily responsibilities.

This is not "keep your friends close, your enemies closer." You want a true connection with the person who has the ability to replace you. They are not a threat. They are going to help you make your business thrive, grow, and earn even more revenue.

If you have a real connection with this person, then they have a different motivation for stepping in and helping you. If they were your frenemy, then they would constantly be trying to show you up. But if you're a team, then you make each other look good. You are helping your future replacement grow. Your future replacement is helping your company grow. Win, win.

Protect your replacement. Stand up for them. Be honest with them. Give them the feedback they need. Finding your replacement helps you be more hands-off, so you can be thinking even more about the big picture for the organization. It's not about putting yourself out of a job. You're carving a new role for yourself. Cultivate a relationship of trust so you have someone who will have your back.

Finding a mentee doesn't mean you've made it. It just means you are more willing to fail in public and that you're ready to step up for your company. You never know when you're going to need to step up. Don't wait until you get a promotion (or a new role) to start grooming someone to take your place.

CHAPTER 8

STEP UP

DO YOU HAVE ONE OF THOSE MEMORIES WHERE, EVERY TIME YOU THINK about it, it makes you feel a little bit smaller? You're like, "Oh, *God*, why the fuck did I *do* that?!" You're just completely mortified with yourself—you know those? This is one of my horrible, cringeworthy memories.

A while back, I ran a company called FrontSide, another software-as-a-service company. FrontSide, the product, was meant to be a small, individually worn telemetry device that would provide an extra dimension to athletes, like an Apple Watch but cooler and better. The genesis of that was a project that we did at SquidWorks for the US Navy, which was an underwater navigation device. Imagine a ruggedized iPad that could go in the water with the latest version of Google Maps. Navy SEALs and marines could pre-program missions into them, and then they could navigate the water, which was a problem that loads of engineers have tried to solve with varying levels of success. It's another SquidWorks-ism: all these big companies tried to solve the problem, but we, little ole us, ended up doing it, and it was working reasonably well.

I looked at what we had made, a feat of three-dudes-in-a-shed engineering, and spoke to a couple of friends of mine who were into scuba diving. We kicked around the idea: "Hey, we've done all the military-grade engineering. Let's make it a consumer product." We worked together, spent our savings, and came up with a concept, industrial design, and product design.

I reached out to an old contact that I'd had, the guy who invested in BombaWorks.[14] I said, "Hey, I've got this idea. It's a little bit related to what we were doing at BombaWorks, but it's action sports vertical. We've worked out some pretty cool tack; we could visualize this on top of GoPro footage of skiing, and it would tell you how fast the person was going, all of this extra data, without adding another layer of convention to the content."

I'd helped them build a demo of their product at BombaWorks that I then took to a manufacturer who I'd worked with before in China. I had proven myself to this guy, and so he said, "Sure, how much money do you want?"

We asked for one and a half million bucks, and he agreed, no questions asked.

We did a term sheet, which is the agreement that communicates the details of the deal: "I'm going to give you $1.5 million, and you're going to give me X percentage of the company or X number of shares."

---

14 He didn't come from a tech investment background; he came from waste management of all things.

We were working through the legal arrangements, but the legal contractor was reasonably ill. He had been battling terminal illness for a while. He came back, after working on the papers for a bit, and said, "Hey, look, this is just going to take me a little bit longer to do the investment than I anticipated because I'm going to go have another round of treatment." We told him to take his time.

Meanwhile, we'd already gotten a little bit ahead of our skis: we'd hired an action sports marketing guy that we knew who actually quit his job at GoPro—an obviously well-paid job—to come and work for us.

With the legal contractor out of pocket—meaning the investment funds weren't yet in our bank account—we had to figure out how to pay the marketing guy. My savings account was not going to sustain someone on a $125K annual salary for very long. We went back to the investor and asked him to spot us some cash until we signed the full agreement. We proposed setting it up as a loan, so if anything horrible happened, where the investment didn't go through, we'd owe him money, but if we went through with the investment, he'd just give us $50,000 less than we originally agreed.

He was really gracious about that, saying, "Look, absolutely, I don't want to lose the momentum on what you guys are doing. Let's go for it." We took the money, and we started paying Andy, the action sports marketing guy. We got into a little bit of a go-fetch game: we operated under the assumption that in two months' time, we'd have the money from the investors—because the $50,000 was only going to last about four or five months.

We kept paying Andy, but then I heard from the BombaWorks CEO that the investor had become really, scarily ill. Very unceremoniously, he told me that the investor had died.

We got into a proper oh-fuck moment: we had already spent the fifty grand we'd borrowed. The rest of the small FrontSide team and I did our best to rally quickly: "Okay, we have less than a month's worth of Andy's salary in the bank..." We went into heavy-duty damage control—and panic mode. We had to grind everything to a halt because we didn't have money. We had to tell Andy that basically the job that he signed up for wasn't a job anymore because there wasn't money anymore, so there wouldn't be a product anymore. These messages came as quite a shock to him; he'd been living in San Diego, and he moved to LA to be closer to his new work. It was a bit of an upheaval for him, to say the least.

Eventually, we got to a point where we had to call this thing. It was over.

The worst part about this isn't that the business failed. That sucked because I really believed in that product and that company's vision. We had a cool website, we had a logo, and we had a marketing plan, but we had nothing that resembled a prototype by that point. I'd also had to write some personal checks to keep the lights on. To tide Andy over in his last month of employment, I had to dip into my personal savings account and drain the battery completely. I was out $66,000 to cover Andy's paycheck and to pay back the loan. But at the end of the day, I was fine because I was doing PiedPiper stuff more and more. I had something *else* that I loved to fall back on—but this poor guy who completely uprooted his life to work at our company...that's a failure that's tough to deal with.

Class, Meet Your New Teacher: Flesh Wound

I won't make that mistake again. My bank account was wounded, and my sense of self was wounded, but that's okay—because, off the back of that failure, I actually learned something.

All in all, I had been cut by the experience, but it was a flesh wound. Nothing too deep, no arteries punctured or broken bones; no one really got hurt. We didn't take any money from little old ladies or steal from Firemen's pension funds and lose it on hookers and blow. It was definitely not the worst Silicon Valley waste of investment, but it was humbling.

It wasn't our fault that the investor died, but it was our fault that we spent money we didn't have yet. Ultimately, that's what got us into trouble. We had a vision for the future, and we never stopped gazing at that imagined big picture to come up for air and say, "Wait a second, we don't actually have any money in the bank. How's about we hold off on this for a while?" Worst of all, we did the thing I hate, which is spend money on things that didn't really matter. We were basically dumping money on whole-price Herman Miller chairs. We started working on the branding because we knew we wouldn't get an invoice from the agency until the funding came through. Instead, we should have waited six months until we could pay the agency to work as fast as possible, not as flexible as possible.

Flesh wounds are powerful teachers. They reinforce the lessons you've been learning on your way to this moment in time.

After I found out FrontSide was screwed, my first instinct was to negotiate down the debt as opposed to jumping from the roof of the nearest tall building. It wouldn't have occurred to me that I could negotiate my way out of a financial bind two years prior. Now I can look back and say I did everything I could have to make that situation right. I fought for that company. I made some mistakes, but it's because I made those mistakes that PiedPiper is thriving so much. I didn't let that mistake happen in vain. I learned from it.

What Does It Mean to Step Up?

"Stepping up" has two definitions: it's getting up when you've fallen down, and it's filling a void of leadership when one opens up. Either way, it's about making yourself vulnerable.

To learn from your failures, you have to stop long enough to look at them. And that's scary. If you're the kind of person who tells yourself that you *are* bad if you *did* a bad thing, you're going to have a harder time reflecting on the memory of that failure. But the thing is: you've got to roll back the tape and watch the replay. You need to see what went wrong and take responsibility for your part in it in order to learn from that mistake. It takes guts, vulnerability, and a willingness to get and stay uncomfortable to take a good, hard look.

To fill a void in leadership and become a higher-ranking leader yourself, you have to have the courage and confidence to try, and you have to trust your replacement to do the work you can no longer do. If you appoint someone to fill your old role and they do a fuck-off job at it, then that makes you look pretty bad. It makes you vulnerable to criticism and judgment. That's a tough thing to deal with—especially if, traditionally, you're a people-pleaser. If you can step up in the first-definition sense, it makes it easier to step in the second-definition sense.

How to Step Up

It's not possible to step up unless you have a sturdy foundation—a support system. You have to have a replacement you trust. To learn to trust them, you have to put them into a place of seniority in the organization and be like, "You can do it, chap!" Much like I had to do with Robin when suddenly I was the COO at PiedPiper.

For your replacement to step up, you need to have built a sturdy foundation of people beneath them, people who can step up and take *your replacement's place*. It's not an exact synchronization where everyone just climbs up a rung in the corporate ladder. There are going to be massive gaping holes.

Robin didn't become the VP of operations. He stayed as the director of operations. He's going to get there eventually, but he's also got to step up beyond where he is today to actually bridge that gap. Because he's still doing too many individual contributor comp talks. He's not leading enough because he didn't get exposed to that skill—and part of that is because he doesn't have someone who *he* can hand his tasks to.

He takes on a lot himself. He delegates very specific tasks, but he doesn't enable problem-solving. That happens all over the business. It's true in engineering. It's never going to be perfect.

If you wrote down all the things you could expect at a startup, no one would ever volunteer to do it. Lots of things in life are like that: if you knew what you were getting into, you'd never go forward; you'd choose a safer, straighter path. Startups are horrific because they're not orderly. As humans, we like order, but every single startup goes through failures and, therefore, learning experiences. I said this to the PiedPiper chairman not that long ago: "*My* grad school was having to go through that lawsuit." (Remember that doozy from Chapter 1?)

Being the COO is phase two of my MBA, as far as I'm concerned. We raised money. We ended up with multiples of eight figures in the bank account. Now we have to manage that and hope to God we don't run out of it before we refill the coffers. It's palm-sweating shit. Every two weeks, there's a whooshing sound as a quarter of a million dollars leaves the bank to make payroll and accounts payable. At the end of every month, we wave goodbye to $500,000.

When you step up into a leadership role, you're suddenly in a place where the numbers are very big, and you have to make *decisions* with those big numbers. One-hundred-thousand-dollar decisions, not ten-thousand-dollar decisions. (Insert cartoon gulping sound.) How do you deal with that?

You need to get assistance from a team of people you trust, people with the skills to help you. You need to always be learning, always humbled. You need to get comfortable with injuries to your pride—with failure, judgment, and self-doubt. You do that by minding your own damn business (literally) and averting your gaze from the big-tech companies and their front-page success stories.

Robin's going to need to step up and take things on, manufacturing-wise. We're constantly waiting for the next step up. The next step up might be the PiedPiper board saying they want me to be CEO (though I'm positive that won't happen any time soon—don't worry, Ed). Terrific. I'll gladly take that on, even though that looks a lot like an awfully tall building. It's tough to climb and even more dangerous to fall from.

Stepping up is not about changing your job title. It's making sure you maximize the opportunities that are presented to you and knowing that you're probably going to inflict more pain on yourself in the process. And that can be a good thing if you let it be.

Dust Yourself Off and Step Up

Yes, I failed. But then I tried again. Desensitize yourself against failing, so it doesn't sting so much when it happens. Decrease the mourning period, get back out there, and step UP.

While you are getting shit done, don't lose sight of the big picture. Get *more* comfortable being uncomfortable—and come back to that state of being again and again.

As you have to step up, you are giving others the opportunity to step up too. As outlined in the previous chapter, identify and prepare your replacements and their replacements;

you want someone who is eligible for leadership to feel ready for leadership.

Finally, make sure you maximize the opportunities that are presented to you but get ready for *more* pain and hard work, not less. You will fail. Know this. You are going to fail a lot. You may have a failed company. A failed product. You may hire the wrong people with the wrong specializations. There's no time like the present—all these clichés exist for a reason. Move fast enough to fall down because it's when you get back up that you learn the most.

CONCLUSION

YOU'VE GOT TO REALIZE YOU HAVE A LOT OF CONTROL OVER YOUR OWN destiny, regardless of your starting point or your perceived setbacks. It's okay that you didn't start from money. It's okay that you don't have that Ivy League education and a bunch of letters following your name. It's okay that, right now, your team is small. You can still achieve all your business goals and—dare I say it?—*dreams*. The only part of the business equation that's essential to success is discomfort. You have to get comfortable being uncomfortable because it's in those moments of discomfort that you'll find original solutions to your unique business problems.

Throughout the book, you've learned how to get shit done, how to work and vacation like the rich (even if you're not), how to scale with intention, how to create an ideal company culture, how to lead and create a new wave of leaders, and how to then go forth and do the thing. Here's a brief montage of the lessons:

How to Find Your Asymmetric Advantage

Your competitors' goals are to replicate procedures or processes because they're thinking the same way you were before you read this book: if a process works in one place, why wouldn't it work in our place? By now, you've learned that without the contextualization of *why* that process is being used, you might not understand how to implement it effectively. The process might've been implemented in one organization because they had a systemic problem to address, one that was unique to their situation.

If you think of a startup as a giant science experiment, then you're working on a hypothesis when you're launching your company and building your product. The question you have to answer is, "Is everyone going to really care about these things that we're doing?" Sometimes, the answer is a wildly exciting, resounding *yes*. Sometimes, a billion people really care about it, and it's tingly and amazing. And sometimes, no one gives a shit about it.

If you focus on your asymmetric advantage, reassessing your assumptions about people, money, and experience, then you're gold, Ponyboy.

I look at what we were able to do at SquidWorks with massive affection these days, but we didn't have a pot to piss in. We had so little money that it was just absurd; we lived a hand-to-mouth existence. But it meant that we pushed ourselves to do things that we ordinarily wouldn't have done. We used our supposedly poor circumstances to our advantage.

How to Get Shit Done

The issue of paralysis by perfectionism at BombaWorks was something that frequently occurs in a beginning phase organization: the sales guys were selling magic tricks they couldn't perform yet. Just whatever sounded great. The CEO thought, "I have an extraordinary group. These folks can do anything. I'm simply going to sell whatever I can get away with selling, and essentially, we'll work it out." If you can actually do it, you should go sell the fantasy in light of the fact that the fantasy is more achievable to your tech-related startup than different kinds of new companies. You have designers and engineers working for you: you might as well tell people you've got actual breathing unicorns on your team. But remember: working in tech has all those magical flourishes, sure, yet it isn't exactly magic. Consider your team's human limits and the restrictions to the fantasy you're selling. Now, go off and work out how to sell that amazing thing you have (or almost have).

"Move fast and break things" is the startup mantra for a good reason. It very well may be frightfully awkward for a few—or in any event, for most. Many times, the mantra can function admirably; in others, it can sink the organization. At the point when you can discover the balance, that's the point when the sorcery really shows itself in your business. You can't effectively run an organization until you figure out how to get shit done.

How to Balance the Pressure

When you're going, going, going at your startup, it's easy to get burnt out. To ration my energy, I'll combine a few tactics: I'll get the hell out of my office (or away from my dining table, these days), avoid burnout by honoring my personal boundaries, and practice monk time.

I live about five miles from the Golden Gate Bridge, and I'll walk from my house to the bridge and turn around and walk back sometimes. I don't do this *every* time I have my little digital-detox monk time, but I have done it before, and it's been refreshing for me. That walk will take me four or so hours, depending on how many shops I poke my nose into on the way through the neighborhood or how quickly I want to walk up a hill.

That helps get the fog out at some level, doing something that resembles exercise—that's not necessarily why I do it, but it's a nice by-product. Walking for ten miles isn't the worst thing in the world for you. My time away from the office is time that I can catch up on podcasts that I actually want to listen to and that aren't necessarily part of my daily routine. It'll be one of those podcasts where someone said to me, "Hey, you should check this out sometime. It's really cool." Boundary-setting makes it possible for me to have several hours to myself during the day.

How to Create a Winning Culture

Culture is something that you make, something you have to be gentle with. It scares easily. But on the other hand, there's toxic culture too, something that creeps up unexpectedly, so now and then, culture is something you need to scrap and reproduce.

Culture isn't written with a capital *C* until you have a sound number of employees, yet it exists from Day One.

Everybody thinks culture implies smiling employees sitting at their desks or playing Ping-Pong in the break room, yet it's really everything: the cycles, the perspectives, the actual work. It's the people who make up your business. Do they feel like they can call anybody they need to if there's a real emergency? The response to that question says a ton regarding your organizational environment.

Develop a culture where camaraderie can happen naturally; don't force closeness with obligatory gatherings and phony team-building exercises. Comprehend the contrast between what is significant to your organization and what is important to your colleagues.

Also, get this: you can't scale culture. There's no scaling the business and going, "Goodness, we're astonishing. We've got this business with a hundred people, so now we have culture." You need to ensure you have a strong culture among the OG crew at your company before you begin bringing new individuals in.

How to Scale with Intention

Look for people who share your values and hire them to work at your organization. You need people with comparable cares and concerns to help you bring your dream to life.

Have the self-awareness to expand the company at the right time. What choices might you make today that will get strengthened at the subsequent stage? Is purchasing IKEA office furniture the best strategy for making room for new people? Ensure that while you're thinking ahead, you don't lose track of the main issue at hand. If you're not a public organization yet, don't act like a public organization yet. Just because you have the cash to recruit new people currently doesn't mean you need to.

It's okay to keep wearing different hats for a while. Don't get too big for your boots. Figure out how to appropriately scale and inspire your group.

How to Lead People

There are times when I believe we aren't doing certain things very well at PiedPiper, but it's not my department. They're not my people directly, so getting involved to reorganize something isn't really going to help because I'm not going to be managing those people long term. I don't know the full history of working with those people, nor do I have any intuition as to how they'll react to certain changes.

Because you don't operate inside those teams as an integral part of the culture, it means that you don't have a three-sixty view of what's going on. It's like commenting on someone else's relationship. You only see the outside. You can be silly in private, but in public, you're really serious. And people go, "Oh, well, those people are so boring. They're so uptight." But then maybe behind closed doors, they're a bunch of clowns.

That's how things are at the big-tech companies too. They only show the side they want you to see; they're not giving up their real leadership secrets.

When we remember that the foundation of the culture is a precious thing that happens organically, then we'll realize we're trying to implement organizational efficiency at the cost of the most precious thing that we have in the organization, which is the whole team. Lead your company with honesty and authenticity and make room for growth. It's in your best interest.

How to Find and Train Your Replacement

Find someone who can replace you and train them like they're headed for the Grand National. Lean on them to make you better.

Find someone who is a younger version of yourself, or maybe they could remind you of someone very close to you. See their potential but also recognize their shortcomings. Determine if you are the person who can help them. If so, do. Take them from bad to better; don't worry about going from good to great. You're not an expert of "good to great," so don't pretend to be. Helping your replacement get from "bad to better" will help you achieve greatness.

When you train your replacement, you have to let them take the lead on a certain project—so you are acting as *their* replacement, their backup. Let go, knowing that they will likely mess up (they're learning and growing!); you have to get comfortable being uncomfortable.

How to Get Back Up

Look, not every decision that I made is 100 percent correct. I try to be decisive, and I try to weigh up both sides of the decision, but sometimes, things go wrong. That's inevitable. However, whether or not you get back up—whether or not you *step up* to the challenge is your decision.

Hopefully, you can learn from my mistakes, and there's some wisdom to be gleaned in the previous eight chapters. Now, you can go off and fight whatever battle you've got to fight, whether that's starting your own startup, stepping up inside your organization, or trying to take it to the next level.

Put the Book Down and Do the Damn Thing

Not everything has to be a home run. You can hit a lot of base hits to get the same result. (One million-dollar company makes the same amount as ten hundred-thousand-dollar companies.)

My main goal in writing this book is to get you to stop. Stop doubting yourself. Stop looking for solutions outside of yourself. Stop picking up business books, hoping to find the secret of starting and running successful businesses.

Yeah, you read that right: stop reading books. I mean, don't stop reading books *forever*, but stop reading books *before* you tackle the thing that's right in front of you. The time is now. This is your moment. GO.

You've made it through the book, so put it down, put on your big boy (or girl, or nonbinary) pants, and go off and do the thing. It's probably going to feel really uncomfortable, but that's okay because if you've learned nothing else in the process of reading this book, it's how important discomfort is to your success. If starting, building, and running a killer business is the thing you want to do—if you're the only person in the world who's trying to do this very different and unique thing, then it's going to feel uncomfortable, and you're just going to have to get used to that, one way or another.

So, go! Get out of here! Go get 'em, tiger. Or [insert statement here that will get you to put this book down and sit with your discomfort].

ACKNOWLEDGMENTS

WRITING A BOOK IS NO EASY FEAT, BUT I WENT OUT AND DID THE DAMN thing. I took a dose of my own medicine and made myself comfortable with being uncomfortable long enough to get these thoughts onto the page. I couldn't have done this without the help of some pretty amazing people in my life. Thank you to:

Letícia, my amazing wife, for your support, advice, and encouragement throughout the whole writing process.

My mother, for your encouragement and bestowing your experience upon me, and letting me make some horrible mistakes along the journey to get here.

Amanda and Barbara, my editors, for your perspective, guidance, and hard work in getting my thoughts down. You helped make them cohesive in this book. Thank you for not being afraid to challenge me.

The extended group of Sumos, the greatest creatives, marketeers, and sparring partners I've had the pleasure to work with in so many different stages of my career.

Phil and Rob, who took a gamble on a young guy destined to come to Silicon Valley to change the world. In doing so, you changed my world, and I think we're forever changed as a result!